How Leaders Learn

How Leaders Learn

CULTIVATING CAPACITIES FOR SCHOOL IMPROVEMENT

Gordon A. Donaldson, Jr.

Foreword by **Roland S. Barth**

TEACHERS COLLEGE PRESS

Teachers College, Columbia University
New York and London

Published by Teachers College Press, 1234 Amsterdam Avenue, New York, NY 10027

The account of a CCT meeting in Chapter 8 is adapted from "Sharing the Challenges: Critic-Colleague Teams and Leadership Development," by G. A. Donaldson, Jr., in *Making Learning Communities Work: The Critical Role of Leader as Learner* (pp. 21–28), edited by R. van der Bogert, 1998, San Francisco: Jossey-Bass. Copyright 1998 by Jossey-Bass. Adapted with permission.

Library of Congress Cataloging-in-Publication Data

Donaldson, Gordon A.
   How leaders learn : cultivating capacities for school improvement / Gordon A. Donaldson, Jr. ; foreword by Roland S. Barth.
      p. cm.
   Includes bibliographical references and index.
   ISBN 978-0-8077-4854-1 (pbk : alk. paper) — ISBN 978-0-8077-4855-8 (cloth : alk. paper)
   1. School administrators—Training of. 2. School management and organization.
3. Educational leadership. 4. School improvement programs. I. Title.

   LB1738.5.D656 2008
   371.20071'1—dc22

                                                                           2007045040

ISBN 978-0-8077-4854-1 (paper)
ISBN 978-0-8077-4855-8 (cloth)

Printed on acid-free paper
Manufactured in the United States of America

15   14   13   12   11   10   09   08   8   7   6   5   4   3   2   1

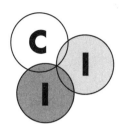

Contents

Foreword

When he was in his eighties, that fearless pioneer Daniel Boone, was asked, "Mr. Boone, were you ever in your life, LOST?"

Whereupon the great explorer is said to have replied, "I can't say as ever I was lost. But once, for five days, I was mighty BEWILDERED."

As developers of leaders in our profession, we may not be lost but we sure are "mighty bewildered." We know all too well how leaders do NOT learn (much):

> From staff development provided by the central office
> From workshops offered by professional associations and
>   consultants
> From university preparation programs
> From state department of education mandates
> From a personal reading of the literature

Despite the best efforts of these and other providers, leaders report that they learn discouragingly little through these means that has a helpful, lasting influence on their leadership.

Yet, for leadership developers, there is much to celebrate these days: The world has begun to recognize that if schools are to significantly improve, it will be the resident practitioners who will improve them. And we have learned that most teachers and administrators have the capacity to develop and provide capable leadership to improve their schools—if the conditions are right. It remains for us to discover those conditions under which school practitioners become voracious, lifelong learners and accomplished leaders.

So how DO leaders learn? Gordon Donaldson, after years of working in the crucible of leadership development in Maine and around the land, has some darn good ideas. Indeed, few have gleaned more valuable insights from their work. The tidy little volume you are about to encounter succeeds admirably in disclosing the conditions Donaldson has uncovered that have led scores of school people to profound levels of personal and professional development.

I have read carefully the pages that follow. But unlike you perhaps, I have also had the opportunity to visit and observe Gordy at work. From his founding of the Maine Principals Academy a quarter of a century ago to his current engagement with cohorts of teacher leaders and school administrators, let me assure you, he "walks the talk." Indeed, I wish the educators who were given the unenviable charge of educating ME many years ago in a one-room schoolhouse, here in the State of Maine had access to his insights. Who knows how I might have turned out!

You will discover in these pages that leaders learn to lead not by studying about leadership, not by attending classes, not by engaging in case studies, not by observing other leaders. Leaders learn through their own practice, by ATTEMPTING to lead. And through careful analysis of those attempts. And by extracting the learning from each attempt. And then by attempting, once again, to lead.

In short, we learn from experience—but only if we REFLECT on our experience. Learning from experience is not inevitable. We know all too many educators who have had the same experiences hundreds of times and have learned little from them. Only to repeat next September what they did last September. Learning comes from experience only when accompanied by intentional, rigorous, fruitful reflection.

The gift of this book is the fine and rich detail it offers about intentional, rigorous, fruitful reflection. Here you will find, in exquisite detail, the self-portraits, the voices and the stories of a multitude of would-be school leaders, all learning by reflecting on their authentic leadership experiences. Rigor and meaning come from employing a rich conceptual framework of the interpersonal, the cognitive, and the intrapersonal components of learning. And by always searching for evidence of success in leadership through self-reporting, through reports of "the led," and by examining the accomplishment of students.

In our profession, especially, one is a learner and THEREBY a leader. The moral authority of the educational leader comes first and foremost from being a learner. The idea of a leader who does not engage in the most important enterprise of the schoolhouse is as absurd as it is unacceptable. We can only lead others where we ourselves will go.

Ultimately, then, the most promising conditions for school leaders to learn in are:

A person who knows and cares about what needs to be done
A person who doesn't know how to do it

A person who recognizes that he or she doesn't know how to do it
A person who wants desperately to learn how to do it
A person who attempts to do it
A person who learns from the attempts

And the lives of many others depend upon the success of the leader learning how to do it.

That's not a bad definition of a leader. And not a bad definition of leadership development either.

—Roland S. Barth

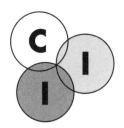 # Acknowledgments

MANY PEOPLE HAVE ENRICHED my education in leadership learning. Their faces, their insights, and our joint experiences have returned to me frequently as I have written this book. I am indebted especially to the many educators who signed on with the Maine Academy for School Leaders, the Maine School Leadership Network, and the University of Maine thinking that I, among others, would be *their* teacher. I will be forever grateful for what they taught me!

Three special colleagues have traveled with me on the 15-year learning path that informs *How Leaders Learn*. I will never be able to separate their learning from my own, nor their contribution to my learning from my own. George Marnik, Sally Mackenzie, and Linda Bowe (who coauthored an earlier version of Chapter 7) deserve extensive credit for the ideas in this book. My deep thanks to you, fellow travelers, and to Dave Brown, Richard Ackerman, Dick Barnes, and Anne-Marie Read, who contributed to both the action and the action research that undergird this book.

And special recognition goes to Joanne Isken, principal in the Los Angeles Unified School District, for her insistence that I write "that I-C-I book." Joanne has been the Jiminy Cricket on my shoulder throughout this journey. I hope the product is as useful to her and her compatriot principals and teacher leaders as she hoped!

As always, I have been buttressed by the enthusiasm and support of Brian Ellerbeck at Teachers College Press, for another project that seeks to serve both practitioner and academic audiences. Kudos to my last-minute graphic artist, Helen: you dressed up my figure(s) just in time! And finally, to my mostly silent and ever-so-patient travel partners through yet another book—Cynthia, Shobe, Clark, and Werther. Thank you.

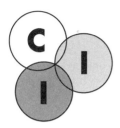

Introduction

LEADERSHIP IS ALL ABOUT performance. We know when leadership is at work in a school because we see leaders taking initiative and we feel mobilized by their ideas and energy. *Learning to lead is all about learning to perform* among our colleagues so that we collectively are moved to think and act in ways that improve how students learn. Those of us who teach leadership, however, haven't often taught in ways that help educators to perform as leaders.

In this book I share lessons from a 15-year exploration of ways to cultivate leadership as a performance capacity. My colleagues and I in Maine created a leadership development program in the early 1990s and, since then, have taken 12 cohorts of educators through variations of that program. Two principles guided us: Learning would be learner centered and developmental, and the test of leader learning would be discernible improvement in student learning in their schools.

These have been daunting principles to follow, as the stories in this book will show. Yet they are responsible, in large part, for the success of our innovative programs. The principals and teacher-leaders entering our programs responded to the idea that their learning—not our teaching— was the central arena of the experience. Our emphasis on looking for evidence of leadership in student learning, though very ambitious, squared with their own reasons for seeking leadership roles: They came because they wanted to learn to perform in ways that "make a difference for kids." The many learning journeys sampled in this book, then, navigate the "complex links," as Hank Levin put it, "among leadership, school functioning, and student learning" that are essential to effective leader performance (2006, p. 43).

I introduce a model for leader learning that helped us all chart the waters through this complexity. From listening to our fellow educators engage in learning, it was clear that their success hinged on how their colleagues at school responded to their efforts. These colleagues were the central actors; learning to lead was all about how to relate with them to stimulate productive work. It was equally clear that learning to perform as a leader sparked numerous "inner dialogues"—questions prompted by changing relationships, a changing role, and growing insights about school improvement. We eventually formalized the two aspects of leadership learning as the *interpersonal* and the *intrapersonal* domains. These became two legs, along with the better-known *cognitive* domain, of the Interpersonal-Cognitive-Intrapersonal (I-C-I) learning model that is elucidated in this book. (While our model has become known as the I-C-I model, the summaries and figures in the book present the domains in C-I-I order to reflect the sequence most familiar to people as they come to understand leadership challenges and tasks.)

My goal in writing *How Leaders Learn* was to describe the learning experiences of school leaders and how this model helped them navigate their own paths toward effective performance. I rely heavily on the words of participants in our programs to take the reader inside the learning process. I offer commentary and analysis about these stories to identify lessons that we, staff and participants, have drawn about the dynamics of performance learning. I hope that many learning leaders will find familiar territory here and perhaps gain new perspectives from the I-C-I model for their own search for enhanced performance. And I hope it proves useful to my colleagues in universities and professional development circles—including school district leaders intent on cultivating leadership within their districts.

The leaders you meet in this book are, with the exception of Shirley in Chapter 1, real people trying to make a difference for the students in their schools. They are principals and teacher leaders with widely varying experiences and working in the variety of schools and communities found in Maine. They were participants in the Maine Academy for School Leaders (1991–93), the Maine School Leadership Network (1997–2004), or the cohort graduate program at the University of Maine (1995–present). Their writing—journal entries, Leadership Development Plans, critical incident analyses, feedback summaries from colleagues and faculty, self-assessments, and portfolio collections of "evidence of growth as a leader"—constitutes, along with materials developed by program staff, the raw material for this book. I used standard coding procedures to analyze these materials for themes related to the learning process and selected a variety of successful cases to illustrate those themes.

Although the I-C-I model gives equal attention to the interpersonal, cognitive, and intrapersonal knowledge domains, in the book I give more prominence to the interpersonal and intrapersonal because these are the lesser known of the three domains. While illustrations and commentary about cognitive growth appear throughout the book, interpersonal and intrapersonal learning are addressed separately, each in a chapter of its own. This emphasis serves to highlight that the "I and I" are complementary to the more familiar cognitive domain: Successful performance results not just from what we know about good practice but largely from how we relate to others and how well we know and can manage ourselves. In my recent work, *Cultivating Leadership in Schools* (2006), I explore more fully the relational view of leadership underlying our learning model.

This book falls into three parts. In the first, comprising Chapters 1 through 4, I portray the I-C-I domains and examine central themes in the learning process. Chapter 1 takes the reader inside the head of a principal at work and introduces the interpersonal, cognitive, and intrapersonal as a useful language for understanding performance and learning. In Chapter 2, I offer three cases of leaders' learning, demonstrating how two teacher leaders and a seasoned principal drew on the model to understand and direct their own learning. Chapters 3 and 4 highlight two central components of the learning process: how ongoing leadership experience is essential to learning to perform as a leader and how real challenges that leaders face in their practice are powerful catalysts for learning.

In the second section I delve more deeply into the nature of interpersonal and intrapersonal learning and into the difficult matter of documenting leader effectiveness. Chapter 5 reveals the challenges and insights gained by our participants as they sought to deepen their ability to cultivate the strong working relationships needed to mobilize school colleagues to improve practice. In Chapter 6, I explain how participants examined vital intrapersonal questions prompted by their learning and leadership experience: How do I know that I am "leadership material"? Do I really want to lead? Where do I "fit" best as a leader: In what roles can I be most effective and benefit the school most? Chapter 7 addresses a vital evidentiary question: How do leaders (or participants in leadership programs) know they are leading? Here, I share participants' efforts to gather evidence from themselves, from colleagues at school, and from impacts on students that their learning efforts are bearing fruit in improved performance.

In the final three chapters, I shift away from the stories of learners and address more directly the conditions for nurturing leader learning and the nature of that learning itself. I identify in Chapter 8 five conditions that foster the kinds of learning illustrated in previous chapters, drawn from our program structures and processes. Chapter 9 provides a more scholarly synthesis of performance learning. I summarize the substance, skills, and dispositions of the I-C-I domains and draw in recent literature on intelligence and on adult and professional learning to elucidate how learning occurs differently in each. Chapter 10 contains my gratuitous advice to leaders, districts, professional associations, and universities, as I encourage them all to take leader development and leadership performance seriously by treating them as core activities in every school and school district.

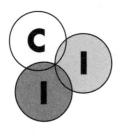

A Language for Leader Learning

WHEN I WAS A NEW PRINCIPAL, I would sometimes sit alone late in the afternoon in my office pondering a particularly difficult dilemma. I remember my mind naturally turning to people I'd worked with whom I thought of as leaders and wonder, "What would Dan do with this? How would Becky respond?" In the years since, I've discovered that this is a common practice among school leaders: seeking guidance from the example of past "leaders I have known."

I've also learned, though, that these models have their limitations. What Dan might have done—and more important, *how* he might have done it—in Philadelphia 12 years ago doesn't translate cleanly to what I should do next in Ellsworth tomorrow. No matter how similar we might think a leader's work is, the context for that leadership is always different, most notably in the cast of characters and relationships among those we seek to lead. And leaders ourselves—our personality, our interpersonal skills—are sufficiently different and unique that how I'd carry out a strategy that I admired in Becky's leadership would likely yield different results from hers. One leader in one school might successfully generate leadership, while another leader in another school might behave similarly but not generate leadership there.

We've learned from this that it's very important to distinguish between ourselves as *leaders* and the leader*ship* we're trying to cultivate in the school or district. Leadership is outside ourselves; it's a relationship that has grown up among leaders and others that produces benefits for students and their learning. Leaders contribute to the growth of this relationship among others. They're continually asking, "Am I generating leadership? Are my colleagues responding to my efforts so that we all improve children's learning every day?" Leadership is about what *we* accomplish. Being a leader is what *I* do.

This distinction is vital to understanding the subject of this book—leadership learning. We can learn what leadership should look like; indeed, we often study images of it from theory and research. But learning how to be leaders necessarily focuses us on how our own actions, beliefs, and personality are playing into the mix of people we seek to lead. We now know that much of a leader's knowledge is not "from the book" but is learned from experience. It is self-generated because this learning is shaped by the leader's unique circumstances—personality, relationships, goals, and school situation. We now recognize that much leader knowledge is "tacit" or unspoken; we learn it not so much by conscious design as we do by attempting to perform it (Sternberg & Horvath, 1999).

In this chapter I introduce a framework for thinking about leaders' learning that we in Maine—and many with whom we've worked elsewhere—have found helpful. It presents learning as a developmental process stimulated by the goals and experiences we have as leaders and enriched by the people whom we seek to lead. As we grapple with our own successes and challenges, we come to understand more fully what we do and to reshape how we will do it the next time. The I-C-I framework offers a language for leader knowledge that can be applied to specific individuals and situations. To introduce it, listen in on Shirley, and her internal dialogue in italics, as she facilitates a faculty meeting. Shirley is the principal of Malden Street Middle School.

A LEADER IN THE MIDST OF LEADERSHIP

"But it makes a lot of sense educationally, Arnie. You've got to agree that it does!" Shirley urged.

"Yes, it can make sense educationally," Arnie responded, "but the real agenda here is political. The state and our own school board want to make us the scapegoat by publishing all this so-called outcome results stuff."

Several other teachers joined in: "Yeah, they're just passing the buck for not funding schools all these years." "These tests don't make any sense; we can't use the results to make our teaching better 'cause it takes 8 months to get them!" "What are we wasting our time on this for, anyhow? I've got more important things to do."

Shirley felt the meeting spinning out of control. *Oh my God, I was afraid this would happen. How am I going to keep us on the agenda?* Simultaneously, the underlying purpose of her meeting turned to a palpable fear: *How am I going to make Dr. Churchill's schedule for implementing these standards-based assessments? I'm getting almost no support from my faculty here . . .*

"We really have no choice about this!" Shirley found herself blurting out. "You know as well as I that the legislature and the governor started this ball rolling 8 years ago. Now the Department of Education is requiring us to report all these measures and Dr. Churchill and our own school board have set these deadlines."

Danette Sparks's hand went up. Danette was well respected on the faculty as a superb teacher and a lifelong member of the school's community. "Can we look at this another way, Shirley? We've put so much into restructuring our curriculum and forming teaching and learning teams in the past 7 years. We've done so much to personalize learning, to address the individual talents and aspirations of each and every one of our kids. I'm worried that all this testing and measuring is going to take us right back to where we were before. Can't we explain that to Dr. Churchill and the board?"

"I've brought that up several times at the A-Team meeting. So did Carlton about his school. Like I said, we've gotta do this." Shirley felt her own frustration rising. She agreed with Danette and knew that the time and energy needed for these state mandates would make it very difficult to maintain their progress in making Malden Street Middle School a place where, truly, all students would grow, learn, and prosper.

Just then, Marcus stood up. He was shaking. "I've had it with this!" he barked. "I'm insulted as a professional by the way we're being treated! What makes a bunch of lawyers in the state capital think they know more about kids than we do?! How in hell do *they* know what should be going on in *our* classrooms? We need to draw the line right here: We refuse to use our meager planning time for their crazy policies when we've got kids right here who need us! Who's with me on this?"

The meeting exploded. "You're right, Marcus!" "Go for it, M!" "It's about time we stopped rolling over and playing dead!" "I didn't get into teaching to be somebody's lackey!"

Think fast, Shirl, old girl. What do I do now? If I stay the course, I'll probably make this worse. "Hold on, hold on . . ." Shirley held her hands in the air, trying to get everyone's attention. "Can we discuss this calmly? Can we talk about this? Remember our meeting ground rules!" *Oh, man. Marcus has lit the fuse and it's burning faster than I can move. What will bring them back?*

A few teachers' arms shot into the air to signal silence and the hubbub began to subside. Sylvia, a seasoned sixth-grade teacher and teammate of Marcus's, broke in, in a loud voice: "We're all just at the end of our rope, Shirley. It's progress-report time, we've got the break coming week after next, and it's just unreasonable to be asking us to do this now. Isn't there something you can do?"

Isn't there something I can do?! How in the world will I be able to get the state, the board, and the superintendent to change their tune? "I appreciate where you're coming from, Sylvia . . . Marcus . . . all of you. I really do. We've all worked so hard to make Malden Street Middle a really great school. But I don't see these assessments as bad. They're going to just show everyone what a great place we are . . ."

Uh-oh. Here comes Marcus!

"I'm sorry, Shirley, if I'm shooting the messenger here, but you can't be serious! With all the work we've done with authentic assessments and differentiating instruction, how can you agree that standardized tests and all this accountability is good?"

Shirley countered with her arguments. Other teachers entered the fray, and the meeting dissolved into many conversations, some loud enough to reveal the disgust of the conversants and some in hushed, discreet tones. Shirley, noticing that it was 3:54 P.M., announced, "We'll take this up again next week. In the meantime, I'll send you all the time lines from the super's office."

Shirley's predicament is pretty typical for principals. She brings to her staff an initiative for which, if it is to succeed, she needs their collaboration. And the teachers (at least the vocal ones) don't agree with the initiative. So Shirley is pulled in two directions: one facing toward Dr. Churchill and the board, to whom she is responsible to carry out policy; the other facing toward her staff, to whom she feels responsible to listen and respond, and possibly to help them do what they see as right and proper. After all, what is leadership if the led aren't following?

LEADERSHIP ON THE LINE

In her capacity as leader, Shirley's thoughts and feelings shape her actions—which, in turn, shape the thoughts, feelings, and relationships of her faculty and ultimately influence the strength of leadership at Malden Street Middle School. The stream of her thoughts and feelings *while she is engaged in leading* determine not only what Shirley says to her faculty but also how she behaves in their presence. This flow of words, postures, facial expressions, and actions indelibly mark the relationships she develops with teachers, both individually and as a group. And it is the character of these relationships that ultimately fashions the type of leader she is for this staff and this school. When feelings are stirred to the level they are here, her responses can put her leadership on the line.

Shirley's in a tough spot relationally in this faculty meeting. She's dutifully carrying out her obligation to her boss (and he to his bosses on the board; and the board, to the state legislature and governor). In maintaining her relationship with her superiors, Shirley has endorsed their standards-based assessment agenda. The problem arises when her faculty disagree with that agenda.

Shirley's relationships with her staff are, we can assume, fairly strong; they have worked together to restructure and improve Malden Street Middle over 7 years and they feel pride in their accomplishments. Now, a policy comes down that appears to run counter to the philosophy and practices they've worked for. And Shirley, incongruously to some teachers, is "bringing it down." Immediately, the collegial relationships Shirley and staff have cultivated seem to be slipping into the background as Shirley repeatedly reasserts the necessity of complying with the new policy.

And how is Shirley making sense of these events as they unfold? Is she able to think fast enough to act constructively in her Janus-like persona? Her thoughts and feelings, as captured in italics above, reveal her anxiety that convincing her faculty on this policy isn't going to be a cakewalk. Eruptions of protest set off emotional eruptions within her: *I was afraid this would happen . . . Oh, man, Marcus has lit the fuse . . . How am I going to bring them back?*

Shirley seems unable to locate an alternate path of action. Despite her internal alarms, she clings to "but we've got to do this." And, of course, the more she reasserts this position, the more teachers feel they need to reassert their protests to it. Luckily, the hour is late and the meeting must end before Shirley and the vocal teachers can move much further into what might become a relational death spiral. She now has time—as do the teachers—to ponder how in the next week's meeting she might approach this issue more constructively (or even how she might use her leadership skills between now and then to make it more constructive).

The aim of this book is to clarify how Shirley and all school leaders can learn to act constructively on the job. Successful leadership in schools is largely the result of thinking on your feet, because leaders in schools ultimately transact their responsibilities face to face with staff, students, and parents. Leadership knowledge is *performance knowledge*; it is knowledge that leaders use while in action. Learning to make sense of leadership situations, to see them as leadership opportunities, and then to fashion appropriate means of acting and being with others are the stuff of effective leadership.

SHIRLEY'S CHALLENGES: THROUGH THE I–C–I LENS

As Shirley ponders what to say and do in the heat of her faculty meeting, she's juggling many factors. First, there are the various players: Dr. Churchill, who determined that ironclad time line; Marcus, Sylvia, Danette, Arnie, and the other teachers who spoke out in opposition; and the less vocal teachers—where do they stand? Second, there is herself, with her sense of duty to the district and superintendent (tied perhaps to her career advancement in the long run), her ongoing relationships with her teachers, and her beliefs about standards-based assessment and their appropriateness for Malden Street. Finally, she faces the immediate matter of the interactions in the meeting and how to respond constructively to both the people and the issues.

How can Shirley sort among these factors and decide how she should act in this setting? Over the past 15 years in Maine, we have been learning about leadership development. We have created a framework for understanding leader learning that has proved useful to many school leaders—principals, teacher leaders, counselors, cocurricular coordinators, even school board members (Donaldson, Bowe, Mackenzie, & Marnik, 2004). We find it helpful because it captures three vital aspects of leadership performance and knowledge: what leaders know about educational matters, what they know about "people" matters, and what they know about themselves.

We call it the I-C-I model for its three domains of leadership knowledge and action: interpersonal, cognitive, and intrapersonal. The framework gives us a language with which to assess leadership demands and successes and to design and pursue new knowledge to improve performance. It has brought us, practitioners and leader educators alike, a new literacy for addressing long-standing deficiencies in leader preparation (Murphy, 1992). Here is how Shirley's predicament is parsed through the I-C-I framework. We start with the more familiar cognitive domain.

The Cognitive Domain

What is the substantive matter lying at the center of Shirley's challenge with her faculty? That is, what educational and organizational knowledge do she and her faculty need in order to work through this dilemma? Here, it's standards-based assessment, a new set of practices for them all and, more than likely, a "black box" of questions for most of them. Critical to Shirley's success is the knowledge base in the room regarding not just standards-based assessment but also organizational change: What is each teacher currently doing? How consistent are those practices across the faculty? What else will need to change to make this policy succeed?

Shirley's own level of knowledge about this nest of topics plays an important role in the situation because she has a lead responsibility. What is Shirley's understanding of assessment in general? Of standards-based assessment? Of how important aspects of it might be learned by her and her staff? This domain of leadership knowledge we refer to as the cognitive. It deals with the leader's knowledge about educational practice, school organization, policy, and the like.

The Interpersonal Domain

While it is standards-based assessment that is generating the heat in this faculty meeting, relational issues are also stoking the furnace. The tacit message from central office is that teachers cannot be trusted to do what is best for kids. People in power have decided that their customary ways of teaching and assessing are broken; and these people are using their power to make teachers change these ways. Even for Arnie, who agrees that the practices should change, the way the message has been delivered is insulting.

This dimension of the situation is all about relationships. Shirley, dutifully doing the bidding of her bosses, has blundered onto thin ice with her teacher colleagues, with whom she has built a robust collegial relationship over the past 7 years. Teachers suddenly wonder about Shirley: "She's never made an ultimatum like this. We've always kicked around ideas first and created our own solutions, using our own judgment. Has she caved to central office?" For Shirley, the challenges here lie in reassuring teachers, maintaining trust, keeping the interactions authentic and constructive.

They call on a second domain of leadership knowledge: the interpersonal. It deals with her skill at understanding the relational issues and at interacting with her faculty to preserve their faith in her and in one another so they together can improve learning for students. We have become more aware of the importance of leaders' interpersonal competence in recent decades as we have confirmed the vital role that emotions and relationships play in leadership success. As Daniel Goleman put it in *Social Intelligence*:

> Leaders need to realize that they themselves set much of the emotional tone that flows through the halls of their organizations, and that this in turn has consequences for how well the collective objectives are met—whether the outcome is measured in achievement test scores, sales goals, or retention of nurses. . . . We need to nurture social wisdom, the qualities that allow the people we connect with to flourish. (2006, p. 315)

The Intrapersonal Domain

A third dimension of leadership knowledge is represented in the vignette by the italicized insertions. These are Shirley's internal dialogues, her self-talk during the meeting. Shirley wonders how she will get the meeting back on track. She becomes aware of a gnawing fear: I might not be able to deliver this faculty for Dr. Churchill. She ponders how to respond to Marcus's anger. She is aware that she has a choice between staying the course of her original—and Dr. Churchill's—goal or dropping back and opening up the meeting to a broader expression of opinions and feelings.

We refer to this third dimension as the intrapersonal. It deals with Shirley's knowledge of herself and with her ability to monitor and manage her thoughts, feelings, and actions in the situation. In a meeting such as this one, where emotions run high, Shirley's feelings cannot help but be engaged; she's feeling pretty vulnerable, squeezed between the demands of her superintendent and those of some of her faculty. Her intrapersonal knowledge includes her grasp of how she's feeling at the moment and how she tends to behave when she's feeling this way. We've all seen leaders speak improvidently in situations like this. Will Shirley know herself well enough to "do no harm" to her relationship with her faculty if she's inclined to speak in anger?

Shirley's intrapersonal knowledge plays a powerful role as she works her way through decisions in her head about the standards-based policy and about what she will say and how she will interact with her faculty. Self-awareness, as Goleman, Boyatzis, and McKee (2002) have found, plays a core part in the exercise of effective leadership. Shirley's success at interacting to maintain a healthy working relationship with her faculty and her success at keeping the idea of standards-based assessment alive hinge on her management of her thoughts, feelings, and ultimately behaviors and words in the meeting. The cognitive and interpersonal dimensions of leadership—the "what" and the "with whom"—are ineluctably connected in the intrapersonal, that is, the "how will I manage myself" dimension.

THE DOMAINS OF LEADERSHIP KNOWLEDGE: A SYNOPSIS

The stories of leader learning in this book reveal how principals, teachers, and others have explored the cognitive, interpersonal, and intrapersonal domains of their own performance. Most important, they depict how these educators came to understand that these types of knowledge have, together, a synergistic impact on their effectiveness as leaders. Planning leadership actions and then enacting them requires the simultaneous use of the leader's cognitive knowledge base, interpersonal sensitivities and skills, and self-awareness and self-management capacities.

A teacher leader, Stephanie Marshall, devised the diagram shown in Figure 1.1 to represent the interplay of the three domains. We call it "Stephanie's Blend" because it reminds us that the more that leaders can draw on all three types of knowledge in leading, the more likely they are to be successful. Leaders who can enlarge their knowledge and skills in each domain *and blend them to make them complement one another* stand a good chance of mobilizing their colleagues to improve.

FIGURE 1.1. Stephanie's Blend: The I–C–I Knowledge Domains

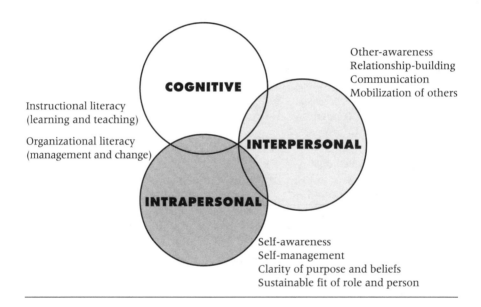

In the remainder of the book I explore this new grammar of leader knowledge and the distinctive means by which learning occurs in each domain. At a time when our profession is seeking a "signature pedagogy" for educational leadership, we think this new language holds substantial promise for both leaders and leadership development professionals (Black & Murtadha, 2006; Bredeson, 1995). I give particular attention to the interpersonal and intrapersonal, the two domains we know the least about and where knowledge is often unspoken and appears largely in enacted forms in performance itself. The two "I" domains, as Howard Gardner (1983) and Goleman (2006) tell us, draw on forms of intelligence differ-

FIGURE 1.2. Core Knowledge Areas of Leadership Performance

KNOWLEDGE DOMAIN	CORE KNOWLEDGE AREAS

Instructional Literacy

- What is effective learning?
- Models and theories of teaching, learning, and assessment for children and adults

Organizational Literacy

- What makes a school effective as an organization?
- Models and theories of school organization, effectiveness, and leadership

Forming Relationships

- How do I cultivate robust working relationships with and among others?
- Skills, sensitivities, and frameworks that help form working relationships with individuals and groups

Mobilizing Others

- How do I mobilize others to act in ways that improve the learning of children?
- Skills, sensitivities, and frameworks that help me generate in others the will and the ability to change

Philosophical Platform

- What beliefs and values guide my work as a leader?
- Core principles with strong rationales regarding the four aspects of leadership listed above

Self-Awareness and Self-Management

- Do I understand myself well enough to choose wisely how I will act as a leader?
- Skills, sensitivities, and frameworks that help me understand how my thoughts and feelings shape my actions with others

Self-Assessment and Career Choices

- Do I understand the assets and liabilities I bring to leadership work?
- Have I found a fitting role that will make my leadership productive and sustainable for both me and the school/team/group?

ent from the predominantly cognitive forms we have typically used in leadership study. In addition, they require different modes of learning.

Figure 1.2 provides a summary of the domains and several subdomains to assist with the chapters that follow. The stories in this book illustrate how the I-C-I framework has facilitated the learning journeys of Maine educators, guiding them toward more effective leadership. As we follow this process, the nature of these seven core knowledge areas will become apparent. Stimulating these journeys were two central questions, "How am I performing as a leader?" and "What can I do to perform better?" The I-C-I framework offered our Maine colleagues, as it has Shirley here, a language for understanding their own leadership experiences. It also gave them a language for framing learning goals and activities that captured the dynamism, relationships, and emotion of their own leadership performance. It gave them, that is, a practical language for their own learning.

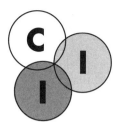

CHAPTER 2

Three Learning Leaders

Leaders are recognized by the people first.
—Wabil Shaq,
former Palestinian foreign minister

WHAT IS THE JOURNEY toward more effective leadership like? In this chapter I describe moments from the stories of three Maine educators who embarked on that journey. Kate, Ted, and Lori signed on to leadership development programs offered in Maine in the early 2000s. The programs—in Kate's case, a master's degree program at the University of Maine and, in Ted's and Lori's, a school-based leadership development program called the Maine School Leadership Network (MSLN)—shared several core elements.

First, they purposely included a wide assortment of educators: teachers, administrators, and other staff, both rookies and veterans, from diverse schools and communities. Second, they were learner centered, focusing on the development of each leader's capacity through a leadership development plan. Third, they were heavily field based from beginning to end. And fourth, they set an ambitious standard for leadership effectiveness: it must be demonstrated in the improved learning of students. (Additional program descriptions are offered in Chapters 8 and 9.)

Kate was a new teacher leader, Lori an experienced teacher leader, and Ted a seasoned high school principal. The snippets of their stories shared here come from the often voluminous writings of learners in our programs. These are reflections on leadership efforts, drafts of leadership development plans, and summary "taking stock" self-assessments done periodically throughout the 2- to 3-year programs. Kate, Ted, and Lori draw on the language of the I-C-I framework to parse out their own leadership activities, assess their effectiveness, and identify learning needs to pursue to enhance their performance.

Because the stories are told largely in the educators' own words, the intrapersonal is often front and center: Feelings, questions, doubts, and moments of new confidence emerge throughout these experiences. And because so much of new leaders' learning is about changes in their relationships with colleagues, the intrapersonal is followed closely by the interpersonal: sorting out where I stand with the principal, wondering how my fellow teachers are reacting to what I just asserted, pondering just how hard to push my own agenda lest I alienate others. Cognitive knowledge is scattered throughout, often in highly specific terms such as a reference to a book, a model, or a reform strategy.

KATE TESTS THE LEADERSHIP WATERS

Kate had 5 years of teaching experience under her belt when she began a master's degree program. An energetic, inquisitive former athlete, she was serving as her middle school's athletic director on top of teaching full time.

Kate opened a reflective journal entry with this quote from Anais Nin: "We don't see things as they are, we see them as we are." Her first 4 months of leadership development work had provoked a journey exploring the connections between her perceptions of those with whom she worked—particularly her principal—and her conception of herself as a leader in her school. As a young, aspiring leader, Kate initially sought to distinguish between seeing her situation "as I am" and seeing it for what it is. Early in the program she discussed her doubts about her readiness to lead:

> Sometimes I feel overwhelmed because I don't know if I could do all the things [that school leaders are expected to do]. I took comfort in a quote from *Becoming Better Leaders* [Donaldson & Marnik, 1995] . . . "Doubt plagued most throughout—about their capacity to lead, about the possibility of ever 'really' influencing the learning of students, about their personal right to influence others, about their stamina to see it all through." I have felt every one of these emotions.
>
> In the beginning I worried that I was too young to be in the [graduate program cohort], that some would think I was some naive whippersnapper who thought she could take education by the horns and set things straight. As I get to know the members in the group more, though, I take ease [in] understanding that any reason you have for being here is OK."

Kate's work as athletic director (AD) thrust her into a leadership dilemma before she was ready. As the basketball season neared, parents made it known to the principal that they were not anxious to have the coach return. The principal, in turn, asked Kate to evaluate the situation, despite the fact that Kate was in her first semester as AD. Communication between Kate and the principal was tentative. Kate felt that there was little support and even less guidance. Finally, as the season was about to begin, the principal fired the coach. Kate wrote:

> In this situation, a coach needed to be fired. However, my principal feared there would be a political backlash if he took action. When he finally fired the coach, he used me as the scapegoat even though I had nothing to do with the decision. So, the only way to get out and maintain my integrity was to quit [as AD] which was difficult because I am not a quitter. . . .
>
> [What I learned from this was] not to get caught up in the political frame because if you're too afraid of confrontation to do your job, you make it a million times harder on yourself. It's much better to address issues sooner rather than later because an attitude of wait and see only brews trouble.

Kate's first formal taste of school politics as a leader became a crucible for her learning. The lessons about her principal's motives and interpersonal style came relatively easily, if not pleasantly: "I loved being the AD and found it to be one of the most rewarding jobs I've had. However, my administrator seriously compromised my trust and respect, leaving me feeling manipulated, used, and unable to follow him." Kate resolved never to lead in this fashion—never to make those she aspired to lead "unable" to follow her because they could not trust or respect her.

But her experience on a grade-level team and as the AD began to shed light on important intrapersonal knowledge as well. She recognized a double-edged quality to her get-it-done approach to leading:

> I get great satisfaction and personal gratification from seeing tangible results but I get exhausted in the process. . . . I thrive off the pure adrenalin of panic, living in fear that I will make a mistake. So I compensate by being readily available, staying in constant contact with the people I'm working with, double-checking plans of action, and smile. I get exhausted, run-down, and emotionally drained in the process.
>
> I need to gain a better balance on keeping work at work. . . . I just need to take an emotional backseat and not fear failing so much. I need to take more of a facilitator role.

Kate's growing understanding of her own inner needs and of how those needs were shaping her leadership work is typical of many of our Maine colleagues' learning. The work of "seeing things as they are" instead of "how we are" became essential in the development of leadership perspective and skills. And much of that work took our colleagues on journeys like Kate's into understanding themselves, into deepening their intrapersonal awareness and their sense of control over their own performance as leaders.

A year later, while Kate led a small evaluation of a program in her school, she developed several goals for her leadership development. Among them was, "I need to work hard to not take on all of the responsibility [for the team's work with the project]. . . . I need to feel OK about asking for help but balance it with not asking too much of them, as we're all busy and this is an extra thing to do." She repeatedly struggled with her desire to achieve "perfection," which made her critical of others, on the one hand, and take on to many of the group's responsibilities, on the other.

So Kate's type A personality, viewed as a "good thing" by many because type A's "get things done," needed to be reined in, both for the good of her team and for her own benefit. In her pursuit of her learning goal, Kate read Sandra Crowe's *Since Strangling Isn't an Option—Dealing with Difficult People—Common Problems and Uncommon Solutions* (1999). Her cognitive explorations into this issue gave her

> some quiet time to reflect on my growth as a leader and some areas that I need to continue to work on. The book reinforced many things for me, most importantly that it's OK if I get frustrated. Difficult people are supposed to cause you stress but I needed to focus on the control I had in the situation (which was a lot more than I thought I had). In this way it was very empowering reading. I found that I was already using some great strategies but found that simple things like monitoring your breathing and making a commitment to journaling helped to find the "calm" within myself.

For Kate, learning about her own leadership was enriched by the crosscurrents of her leadership experience at school: the people she found difficult (including her principal and some colleagues). The opportunity to engage in reflection, to write, and to have discussions with "safe" colleagues in her graduate program allowed her to sort out "what's me" and "what's them." That is, she could begin to understand the complex dynamics of her own role within the interpersonal milieu of her team or her working relationship with her principal.

The deepening of her intrapersonal understanding was enhanced by some cognitive models and "strategies" she picked up through reading. Her ongoing leadership of a team evaluating a program gave her immediate opportunities to try some of these out and to begin to feel that she had some "control in the situation." In other words, she began to understand how she could consciously take leadership action, deploying herself, as it were, for the benefit of her team and its goal.

At the close of the 2nd year of her program, Kate's growing grasp of what it means to assume leadership responsibility was palpable:

> I think I'm wiser, more realistic about how much a leader can actually do, and certainly more humbled about my own leadership aspirations. When I began this program, I was ready to take on the world and couldn't wait to enter the world of administration. Now, I'm much more hesitant about the responsibilities an administrator has and although I feel that I'm stronger and more prepared, I would like to gain more experience teaching first.

TED CHANGES HIS WORKING RELATIONSHIPS

In July 2001, Ted wrote:

> I have always been guided by the belief that an effective school is one in which teachers help identify areas for improvement and that they then dedicate the time, energy, and resources to make those improvements a reality. It is the principal, in the background, who provides the support, the encouragement, the time, the resources, and the occasional push to keep the teachers focused and fueled.

At the midpoint of his leadership development experience in the Maine School Leadership Network (MSLN), this seasoned high school principal came to the realization that his walk wasn't conforming to his talk. It is the kind of discovery that often fueled learning among our participants:

> That belief guided me, but my actions were often contrary. In the past 3 years, my frame of reference for my effectiveness was me and perhaps two to three colleagues. If I was able to keep six or seven balls in the air juggling the many demands placed upon a high school administrator, I was doing OK. If I didn't have too many grievances against me, I was meeting the needs of most of the people with whom I worked. And if the [state achievement test] scores didn't take too substantial a drop compared to years past, then things were fine with curriculum and instruction.

Ted's self-assessment is familiar to many principals. The realities of their positions shape their thinking about what they must do to be successful. Note Ted's performance criteria: keeping six or seven balls in the air, minimizing staff grievances, maintaining state achievement test scores. And note from whom he took his cues: himself and two or three colleagues.

Ted's learning in MSLN engaged him during the first year in examining his school more closely. At his urging, the faculty was assessing its work with students in four areas suggested by Maine's blueprint for secondary school performance, *Promising Futures* (Maine Department of Education, 1998). His own reflections included not only what his staff was doing but also how his staff were (or were not) working together and, most importantly, how *he* was working with them.

From this came Ted's realization that "my actions were often contrary" to his beliefs about how school improvement and leadership work:

> I used to pride myself in knowing the name of virtually every student in my school. It appeared now I had more pride in juggling six or seven balls, dodging complaints from teachers, and maintaining the status quo.
>
> When did my focus change?
>
> My work with MSLN causes me to reflect and to refocus. Being a principal is about getting those people who can bring about the greatest amount of improvement—the teachers—to work side by side with administration so that student learning improves. My MSLN work forces me . . . to examine how I create and manage relationships within my school so we can maximize our efforts toward improved student performance.
>
> Effective leadership means *us*, not *me*.

Ted's leadership development plans from the outset had focused on "building and maintaining trust with my faculty," specifically targeting those "who exhibit blocking behaviors." After lots of "reflecting and refocusing," he now understands that to do this he must examine his own actions, attitudes, and beliefs, not just those of his faculty—and especially not just those faculty whom he viewed as "blockers."

At the conclusion of his written self-assessment in July 2001, he identified some specific ways he planned to learn. Most notably, he's now focused on how this learning will allow him to behave in more effective ways as he goes about his daily work. He reframed one of his three major learning goals by specifying several interpersonal and intrapersonal objectives:

to improve my patience in working with faculty who are intimidated by the work of school improvement; to gain a better understanding of how those fears impact one's willingness to participate in the school improvement process and help those individuals "come on board"; and to balance my personal need to take action with others' needs to process.

And here is how Ted planned to focus his learning activities in the coming year:

I believe I need to learn more about how groups work. Understanding the hurdles a team will face beforehand will allow me to address those problems quicker. Reading material such as Linda Lambert's book [Lambert et al., 1995] will increase my knowledge, but I need to personalize that material. I can't simply use a quote to express my beliefs about leadership—I have to live it. Much more work is needed on my behalf in reframing my Platform of Beliefs on Teaching, Learning, and Leadership to make it truly reflective of who I am and how I function as a principal.

My work this year has resulted in productive discussions by my faculty on the two most important elements of education— teaching and learning. . . . The stage has been set for the hard work of collaboration in improving student performance. The evidence that has been submitted in the appendices [of this portfolio] indicates that.

Ted's conception of his leadership now revolves around engaging his faculty in issues of teaching and learning. He has developed a philosophical "center" for himself—his platform—that has moved his former performance criteria to the margins. And his view of leadership doesn't revolve around himself; it revolves around the faculty and its ability to mobilize to address the four initiatives for improving student learning. Ted's challenge is clear but possibly quite terrifying: He's now got to learn to act in new ways to do "the hard work of collaboration." Central to his leadership development plan for 2001–02 was a commitment to solicit feedback from his faculty on his success in building a stronger, more authentic collaboration with them.

Fast-forward to January 2002. Ted has pursued a strategy of consciously touching base with all faculty in an effort to increase collaboration and what he called "interdependence" between himself and teachers. He has attended many committee meetings but not in the role of chair. He has met one on one with teachers to understand their views and fears.

He has followed the judgment of the School Leadership Team even when his own need to "take action" was telling him to take charge. Most important, he has practiced asking for feedback on how these strategies are playing out among faculty.

In January 2002, he writes that he has learned something important about how he is seen and understood by faculty:

> [I now see that] not all teachers know who I am, that teachers' views of me differ based on their previous experiences with me or their current interactions with me, and that my personality type as an ISFJ (Introverted, Sensing-Feeling [on the Myers-Briggs Type Inventory]) makes it even more crucial that I take the time to talk with my colleagues on an ongoing basis. [This is the only way that] I can get more tuned to what their needs are, how I can assist them in my role as principal, and that they can get to know how I act and why concerning school-related issues.

Ted has come to see how teachers in his high school understand—and misunderstand—him as their leader. He comprehends better how his personality type and his patterns of behavior affect staff interpersonally and how, in turn, this affects their collaboration together. His own learning journey has required him to chart a course between his desire to control and direct and his faculty's need for ownership and authority. He has emerged with a deeper understanding of the "interdependence" of principal and faculty and, most important, with a growing skill set that helps him track how well that interdependence is working so that he might adjust his own patterns of leadership accordingly.

Ted's learning summary intones a new intrapersonal appreciation for what he can and cannot do as leader: "I have always known 'I can't do it all.' Yet I struggled in the past with those individuals who have a greater need for process versus product. Delegating responsibilities, providing guidance and support, building in accountability checkpoints, and providing an occasional 'push' is leadership. And I have found myself this school year feeling very comfortable with 'I can't do it all.'"

LORI GAINS A FOOTHOLD AS A TEACHER LEADER

Lori is a 12-year veteran teacher who came to MSLN with a history of energetic involvement in program change in her elementary school. When she joined the program, however, she felt burned out. Her readiness to volunteer for tasks on the faculty and to initiate new thinking had, she felt, put up a wall between her and some of her colleagues. Their foot-dragging, the outright resistance of some, and her own flagging energies had led Lori to question her "just do it" approach to leadership.

Joining MSLN gave Lori a chance to pause, to read and think about other models of leadership, and to find partners who shared her enthusiasm for improvement and leadership. A year into her developmental journey, she had signed onto a districtwide committee to redesign math curriculum in light of the state's learning outcomes. As she put it, she joined because the effort "needed leadership. People had at first run from it, but there were rumblings now about 'What will the final product look like if we don't have a voice in the work?'" So Lori had signed on.

Through MSLN, she developed a leadership development plan for herself to "try my hand at 'unfreezing' a staff that was less than enthusiastic for change in this area." Her new leadership strategy was to support and inquire rather than come at her colleagues with a template for how they should change—the way Duke coach Mike Krzyzewski, a leader she greatly admired, might bring a clipboard with basketball strategies to a team practice session.

She plunged into the work with her customary enthusiasm, meeting during the summer with another teacher to align the NCTM and Maine Learning Results standards for math learning. And she called colleagues in her own school to share what was happening in the districtwide committee and pose questions. These calls, she felt, were "an opportunity for me to hear the appreciation expressed that 'someone' was finally willing to do this work. There were thanks and praise in almost each conversation. . . . People were happy to be informed about the status of the curriculum development and definitely wanted me to follow up with them as the work progressed." Some of her colleagues agreed to pilot a new math program aligned to the new standards.

The school year opened with staff training in Investigations, the new math program. True to her personal development plan, Lori through the fall "attempted to make regular supporting contacts with individuals and grade level teams" in her school. "This," she wrote, "would also mark the beginning of my informal data collection. After about 4 weeks into the year I checked in with the second-grade team to see which lessons they had implemented and we compared successes and failures. I was able to do the same with the first-grade team, but not with as much depth."

The feedback Lori was hearing from colleagues about Investigations led her naturally to the assistant superintendent and her principal: "I was excited to be initiating a professional dialogue for a change and quickly wanted to share . . . the enthusiasm, efforts, and concerns the staff was having around the piloting of Investigations. The response I received from [administration] was far from what I expected, and it would prove to be one of my first real challenges related to this initiative." The two administrators ignored the "data" she'd brought and instead "challenged each and every concern raised by the staff. It was as if everything I had to say was being diminished and construed as nothing more than sour grapes and lack of time with the pilot. I wasn't sure what to do next."

Her next steps became a new focus for Lori's learning in MSLN. Her program colleagues and facilitator helped her to think through her goals as a leader in the math effort in light of her hurt feelings and sense of betrayal. Rather than let the interchange with the administrators deter her, Lori continued to meet with the teacher teams, although she "wasn't sure why I was asking these questions and taking the time to meet with teachers individually or in small groups if it served no greater purpose in supporting this initiative." But then she found a deeper commitment in this work:

> That's when it hit me that the greater purpose may not be about what this does for a curriculum coordinator, a school board making decisions about programs, or a math preview committee. The greater purpose may be in what opening this kind of dialogue does for the teachers and their students.

Lori redoubled her efforts with her colleagues, excited by this new conception of her leadership responsibility—taking on her work as a facilitator of dialogue and learning, not as an emissary of the administration or a promoter of her own vision. As if feeling new confidence, she approached the curriculum coordinator to promote an evaluation of the Investigations pilot that would use both the qualitative data she was gathering from teachers and some pre- and posttest measures.

In January, Lori was buoyed by her new mission to work directly with her colleagues. Ironically, the skepticism expressed earlier by her principal intensified. Lori came to see these as "territorial outbursts." Confronted with interpersonal tensions, she chose to "steer clear of these kinds of reactions" and, later, "to diffuse the situation . . . with clear explanation of my plans and by calling her attention to past e-mails or conversations the two of us may have had around the area of concern." It seems that Lori's success as a leader with her colleagues had threatened her principal.

While these events were palpable evidence that Lori's leadership was having an impact, it wasn't entirely the kind of evidence Lori had expected. As is often the case in leadership, progress in changing practices and relationships was making someone in power uncomfortable. Lori's newly revised leadership development goals in January focused on continuing her facilitation skill growth as she worked with her colleagues; these included the following: "I would like to try an approach with the lone teacher who did not participate in the summer math training yet continues to be the most negative individual with respect to the math preview and Investigations program."

Regarding her principal, Lori's leadership plan concluded:

> I would like to focus on one intrapersonal goal: recognizing that her issue is not about me or my work. I want to be able to take my immediate emotions out of play when the principal reacts in a negative way towards something. . . . This may also be about avoidance, so I will certainly be seeking the support of my [small MSLN learning circle] and other cohort members in facing this issue.

FOUR THEMES IN LEADER LEARNING

Kate, Ted, and Lori help bring to the surface some themes in leadership learning. I highlight them here to introduce them for further exploration in the coming chapters.

Uncertainty About How Leadership Works

These three leaders seemed to mull constantly, even as they made energetic efforts to lead, the question, "What does effective leadership look like for this school?" Each was aware that leadership was defined in a number of ways. It was (a) partly shaped by what staff members, the community, and the administration expected leaders to do; but it was also (b) defined in articles, chapters, and by "experts" in ways that did not always square with on-the-ground expectations. They were clearer about their goals and ambitions for the school than they were about how to get there. As they submerged themselves in the effort to improve their performance, the complexities of relationships and of gaining access to others and to models of practice made each leader wonder how they could ever judge their own effectiveness.

The journey toward providing more effective leadership engaged Kate, Ted, and Lori in a rich and sometimes frustrating dialogue about how leadership worked in their own cases. They, like many, were sometimes more certain about what didn't work—Kate's principal, Ted's previous concept of his work—than about what was called for. Notably, all three of these learners grew more certain through sustained efforts to lead and to gather evidence of their leadership effectiveness in their schools.

Certainty That Relationships Are Vital to the Establishment of Leadership

Each of these leaders sensed that trust, respect, rejection, acceptance, agreement, and conflict are vital and perhaps inevitable companions of leaders in schools. Why? Because leaders accomplish their work in relationships with others. Those relationships matter greatly to the leader's success. For the two teacher leaders, the relationship to the principal wrapped them around some knotty issues about authority and trust. And for all three, building open and honest relationships with colleagues among the faculty became the central work of improving their leadership.

So the journey toward functioning as a leader became a voyage into interpersonal learning. Coming to see how "the way I approach her" sets off the principal's "territoriality" was a breakthrough for Lori. Here, learning is about how her personal style, her own behavior patterns, and her beliefs and assumptions about the principal shaped the interactions with her principal in helpful and not helpful ways.

The "Action" of Leading Is a Profound Teacher

All these leaders were energized by "doing leadership"—by their direct experience trying to shape the school, the staff, and their practices so children learned better. This "action" generated rich, exciting, and often confusing evidence of what happens when someone tries to lead. Most powerfully, it was evidence of their individual efforts to lead so it became fertile ground for finding out what works for them personally—and what does not.

Doing leadership work, then, is an important condition for learning to perform as an effective leader. Nothing is quite so compelling as a source of lessons and questions as your own case in your own school. These conditions ultimately give life to—or the lie to—the published, more static cognitive and theoretical descriptions of what leadership is and how leaders should conduct themselves. Without the opportunity to perform, as Ted might have put it, he couldn't have "personalized" his own learning.

Acknowledgment That Leadership Is "About Me"

Kate, Ted, and Lori wrote a lot about how they thought, felt, and behaved in the action of their leadership. The 2 and 3 years of the program gave them time to explore their own beliefs and knowledge about learning, about teachers, about how schools work and improve, and about how leadership functions in this milieu. Most important, time and practice showed them that who they are shapes what they do, think, and feel as leaders. So learning to lead became a journey into intrapersonal knowledge, to understanding, as one of them put it, "how I need to behave and think so that colleagues' practice and student learning grow."

Lessons learned along the leadership road benefit from opening up the intrapersonal world. For Kate, recognizing which emotions were playing in herself as she sorted through the coach dilemma ultimately gave her the power to understand what she should do. For Lori, sorting out what was "her" (the principal) and what was "me" in her evolving relationships as a leader gave her the power ultimately to state what she could and could not be responsible for. And for Ted, the principal, the journey was the reciprocal to Lori's but he too emerged with a clearer understanding of how he could best deploy his own influence. Intrapersonal reflection—often with the help of colleagues—brings self-awareness and a new perspective on what each of these leaders can do and be and, as important, what they cannot.

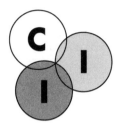

CHAPTER 3

The Lessons Are in the Leading

As soon as you set your course [as a leader],
the winds will come from that direction.
—Jeanne, high school teacher

Be intrepid! Take a risk. The gods protect
beginning sailors and fools—sometimes both
at once!
—Isabel, high school administrator

MOST EDUCATORS ARE FAMILIAR with the theory-practice gap. Most teachers, having endured 4 years of campus-based preparation, notice how different actual teaching is from the way college courses said it would be. Indeed, teaching is extraordinarily in-the-moment work. Students require constant monitoring and deciphering. Teaching techniques prove useful not so much as the manual describes them but as a series of adaptations in response to what students need and are ready for. Teachers learn to perform their art and craft in the rich crucible of their classrooms.

The same can be said for school leaders. Their work calls for planning and preparedness for each day, just as teaching must be planful. But the execution of their work is frequently as person to person in nature as is teaching. Principal leaders respond to people constantly, be they students in need of discipline, parents seeking counsel, teachers requesting an exception, or a planning committee requiring artful facilitation. Teacher leaders' days are filled with individual collegial consultations, team facilitation, and negotiations with administration.

The effectiveness of school leadership lies in how it is performed, not in how it scripted. So leaders' learning often achieves its richest possibilities when leaders can gain perspective on how they operate in action—how *they* performed. In its simplest form, then, to increase your performance knowledge, you need to perform: The lessons are in the leading itself. Brown and Duguid put it this way:

> The central issue in learning is becoming a better practitioner, not learning about practice. This approach draws attention away from abstract knowledge and cranial processes and situates it in the practices and communities in which knowledge takes on significance. (1991, p. 46)

In this chapter I describe how leadership experience takes on significance for learners in our programs: through the power of leadership practice, through opportunities to "see my place" in it, and by focusing on results.

THE POWER OF PRACTICE

Despite the common belief that principals learn everything they need to know *after* they become principals, it took considerable time and effort for many of our Maine colleagues to learn how to learn from experience. They often came to our programs assuming, deep down, that book learning was the primary form of legitimate learning. After all, these educators were successful formal learners—and their livelihoods were wrapped up in purveying more of that formal learning to children.

It took steady pressure from faculty and staff to convince many of these educators that it was acceptable—indeed, preferable—to learn from the action of their own practice. Over time, we developed a number of ways to encourage this process (see Chapter 8). But once individuals found a way to think about their practice that led to deeper understanding, the power of that experience carried them forward to increasingly enriching learning.

Take, for example, Sasha, a fifth-grade teacher in a small elementary school. She had volunteered to lead the staff's standards-based report card effort. An enthusiastic, thorough, and articulate woman, Sasha was nevertheless uncertain about the willingness of her colleagues to follow her lead. She wondered about apparent lethargy in some teachers and possible resistance from others. But it wasn't until she tried to convince her colleagues to do a presentation on the new report card to parents that a new insight into herself as a leader surfaced.

One of her colleagues was, as Sasha put it, "surprisingly defensive": This teacher remarked that she was "planning on doing something on her own with her parents" and was not interested in joining Sasha's school-wide presentation. Sasha wrote:

> My enthusiasm for and belief in the importance of this presentation left me with such a narrow focus that I forgot to pause, step back, and think about the other factors that might be involved. I didn't anticipate Carolyn's reaction. . . . If I had stopped to consider [her feelings] more thoroughly, I may have headed this one off. I strive to be a team player but my thoughts are often on the big picture and not enough on the process or the relationships involved. Then, I'm surprised when people react with what I feel are pernicious and defensive reactions.

This discovery became one incident among many in which Sasha sought to curb her natural inclination to jump to her own conclusions and her own design for action without heeding others' views, feelings, or relationships. Simply having a good idea developed carefully from her big-picture cognitive grasp of assessment wasn't enough. If she didn't conduct herself interpersonally in a productive way, her good idea wouldn't even get a fair hearing. As she sought to change her own behaviors in meetings and one-to-one interactions to accommodate others, she made this observation on her learning: "This was a shift for me. Rewiring myself is a work in progress but one that is updating me to my new codes of effective leadership."

Dinah, a young teacher aspiring to the principalship, sought to influence what she saw as a negative faculty culture at her elementary school. In a series of journal entries, Dinah railed about the negativity of some teachers, describing how their gossip, backbiting, and whining about the principal created a toxic professional climate. Dinah's breakthrough came when she discovered that she was actually a contributor to this climate:

> I sometimes find myself complaining about other people behind their backs. Now, if I were adept at straight talk, I wouldn't do this. However, I keep finding myself in this position, because I don't have the courage to say what I'm feeling about someone to their face. Instead, I vent to a third person and then proceed to "suck it up." Sounds healthy, doesn't it?

Following this realization, Dinah was sensitized to her participation in faculty conversations and discussions. She simultaneously reexamined her beliefs about professionalism and its relationship to her school's success. And from this emerged some goals for her own new behavior patterns at school—goals that engaged her in intrapersonal and interpersonal learning:

I am going to watch myself in this area. I've already been in three situations where I would have reverted to gossiping and whining, but I consciously didn't. I tried to think about what I would have said in the past and how that would have contributed to the conversation. I realized that I would only feed the flames and contribute to the negative conversation.

I didn't leave [the conversation], though. I actively listened . . . and watched the players. I realized that they are really unhappy people! Or, at least, they sounded unhappy. On the other hand, their complaints showed what they valued. The players clearly expressed a desire for good leadership, to have more fun at work, and to know that everyone works as hard as they do. They had really good points, but the conversations they were having won't lead to any kind of change.

Dinah's patterns of behavior—and the attitudes she conveyed—shifted. As she described it, "I am making a commitment to stop involving myself in these kinds of complaining and gossiping sessions. I've identified a colleague who I know doesn't gossip and complain; she's a straight talker, and I'm trying to spend more time with her . . . and use her as a role model." She later documented how in her small school of 14 teachers, some picked up on her shift and how some, including her principal, came to see her as a more influential leader as a result.

While our programs encourage setting goals to stretch leadership knowledge, many of these "learnings-in-action" emerged from the messiness of real life in rather an unplanned way. That's the way it is with experiential learning: it has a quixotic quality, an overtone of epiphany. Insights, as Chris Argyris (1999) and others put it, are "episodic"—they arise out of lived episodes, replete with all their interpersonal, philosophical, political, and intrapersonal realities. Many of our leaders wondered, in retrospect, how they had arrived at their insights. It was, I think, more the result of their openness to the lessons of their immediate worlds than of anything else.

Leadership learning is facilitated by having a plan, a design for learning. But its richest moments are often the result of learners' disposition toward learning—their readiness to value what one experience holds for the next experience. Etienne Wenger, who is among the handful of scholars examining context-embedded learning, put it this way: "Learning cannot be designed. Ultimately, it belongs to the realm of experience and practice. . . . Learning happens, design or no design. And yet there are few more urgent tasks than to design social infrastructures that foster learning" (1999, p. 22).

HEY, THIS IS ABOUT ME!

Thirty aspiring leaders had just witnessed four of their members role-playing a supervisory feedback session between a principal and a not-so-good teacher. The group had debriefed the role-play, focusing especially on the interpersonal style and strategies used by the principal in conveying evidence of subpar performance to the teacher. We instructors had asked each person to write a brief journal entry reflecting on "what, if anything, from this role-play hit home for you."

Suddenly, a gregarious assistant principal who had not been in the role-play blurted out, "Hey, this is about me!" The entire class looked up. One of the instructors inquired, "What do you mean, Victor? How are you finding this to be about you."

"Well, obviously, I'm an assistant principal and I'm in this kind of situation a lot—teachers and coaches who need to be doing their jobs better, even parents who I'm delivering bad news to about their kids. But that's not what I mean, exactly."

"Oh?"

"Well, it's not just that this role-play looks like a situation I'm in a lot. It's that what we were just talking about in the debrief is so much about me. When we were saying that the principal is wondering while he gives negative feedback, 'How is this person taking this? I'm feeling so responsible for [the teacher] here.' Well, that's just exactly what happens to me. And it's why I wonder if I'll ever be a really good principal—or if I really want to be a principal."

Victor had articulated a fundamental principle of leader learning: It's most powerful when "it's about me": When leaders come to understand themselves better as actors within the leadership they aspire to provide, they find essential starting points for improving performance. Ultimately, the instrument of leadership at each leader's disposal is the leader her- or himself. In Victor's epiphany, he encountered himself and posed for himself a central question: If I feel these conflicting emotions when I am acting as a leader, do I really want to lead?

Kate, Ted, Lori, Victor, Dinah. Every example of learning in this book illustrates the "it's about me" principle. Kate, like Victor, found herself reconsidering her goal to be a principal when she discovered her how her own value system seemed incompatible with the way the administrators around her were functioning. Ted, who started out as a principal modeling his practice on the outward trappings of principals he had known, came to the realization that, to really affect the quality of teaching and learning in his high school, he needed to "live" his words, not merely utter them. Dinah's effort to change the climate in her school began with her own intrapersonal "check-in" and her discovery of the ways she was contributing to negativity.

These learners are coming to understand how their daily behaviors, their moods, and their words shape those around them. When they entered our programs, they expected to learn about school effectiveness, leadership and change theory, and management. But now they are seeing themselves as actors in the real professional and interpersonal contexts of their immediate work. Their learning focus shifts to how *they* are shaping the knowledge, attitudes, beliefs, and practice of those colleagues they seek to lead. Deep learning begins with the intrapersonal, with insights "into myself as I try to lead at school." These insights prepare leaders to address their interpersonal performance and learning: "Now, what do I need to do in order to engage others in this work?"

Jeanne's story illustrates a typical transition from thinking leadership was "what principals do" to a more accurate and more organically suited type of leadership that works for her. She's a 28-year-veteran high school teacher who uses biological metaphors to describe her own evolution toward seeing herself as an instrument of change. Importantly, she discovers in the process that she is more likely to succeed as a teacher leader, not as the administrator she started out to become.

"My evolution has a preleadership stage and a leadership stage," Jeanne wrote in her reflective portfolio at the conclusion of her program. She went on:

> Prior to our March Taking Stock session [9 months into the program], I continually questioned why I was in this [program]. I wondered if the district's money was being well spent. I asked myself if this was right for me. I now recognize that I was in my prebiotic phase [in evolution, the period before life appeared].
>
> Something changed in March. From that point on, I realized that I needn't look at school leadership as being the principal or the vice-principal in the building. I could be a teacher leader. Accepting the role of teacher leaders has made a big difference in how I view my role at Glendale High School.

Jeanne then described how she no longer framed her work as department leader in terms of what the administration would or would not allow or how an administrator would behave.

> As a teacher leader I advocate for a change. . . . I have also become involved in a new project in the school, Promising Futures [Maine's secondary school reform initiative]. In the past I became involved

in many activities and initiatives in the school but never felt compelled to advocate and push for my point of view. That has changed! So the preleader phase was wallowing in primordial leadership soup type of activities but now I feel that I have a focus. I now think that I can be a teacher leader. I am entering the biotic or leadership phase of the evolution process.

And in her biotic phase, Jeanne has discovered the it's-about-me principle.

For the past 28 years [as a teacher] I have been comfortable being involved yet staying out of the limelight. I have enjoyed being behind the scenes as a support player but I never took the main role. An incident regarding the Promising Futures grant assured me that I could become a high-visibility/high-credibility leader.

While I think that I prefer the first style, becoming a leader will mean that I move more into the second style. When I led the informal informational meetings [on the grant], I felt seen as well as heard. While the end result, the 88% support of the grant in the faculty, may not have had anything to do with the informational meetings, I found that I was comfortable taking a stand in front of a large group. This was a big change from the behind-the-scenes player of the past.

Jeanne's next leadership development plan formulated steps to guide her practice of this new "high-visibility/high-credibility" leadership. In the best traditions of adult learning, she had made her learning her own and the result was a more authentic and more personally fulfilling understanding of how her own performance might actually contribute to her school.

At the heart of the discovery that learning to lead "is about me" lies the intrapersonal domain of leadership. Victor was acknowledging the realization that how well he leads is a function of how well he knows himself. And how he can use his self-knowledge to, as Jeanne would put it, become a high-visibility/high-credibility influence on his colleagues. This discovery, for these two as for many others, unlocked a new and potent territory for learning and self-development.

KNOWING THAT I AM LEADING

A persistent conundrum in the learning leader's journey is knowing "when I've arrived." What tells me that I *am* a leader? How will I know? The answers to these questions are elusive: You feel you're about to grasp them, and then they drift out of reach, again and again.

Our Maine colleagues grow frustrated with the search for answers to this question. But *asking the question* is perhaps the most important of all leadership habits. Our advice to our leader colleagues boils down to two points:

1. You alone cannot verify whether you are "a success." Only those you lead—or lead with—can know that you are leading. So look to your colleagues and constituencies if you want to know if you are, in fact, doing so!
2. The proof of a school leader's success lies in demonstrable evidence that children's learning and development in the school are improving. Leadership is about more than perception—yours, your colleagues', your employers'. It's ultimately about the bottom line, and the bottom line is that all students are learning and growing in healthy ways.

Our leadership development programs scrupulously avoid constructing a single template of an ideal leader (despite the pained and vociferous demands of some of our participants!). Rather, we try to support all participants in exploring these two principles through their own leadership performance. We say, "Leadership is not in a book or a magic bottle. It's in how you are able to mobilize yourself and others to do good things for kids' learning."

The proof, then, lies in tracing the connections between "what I did" and "benefits to kids." Making this case, however, is often difficult. Improved learning takes time, student evidence, and persistence. To establish a cause-effect relationship between teacher practice and student gains is hard enough. Tracing such a relationship to a leader's performance seems downright impossible.

Our approach to this conundrum is to declare that leaders have no choice in the matter: They must seek evidence that they are making a difference and use it to improve. As I explain in Chapter 7, participants in our programs drew from three types of evidence: their own observations that others were responding to their efforts, feedback about their leadership efforts from their colleagues, and data on changed practices and student gains. The following examples offer brief illustrations of how some Maine educators went about this important process.

The payoff for many of our learning leaders comes when they sense that their colleagues are seeing them as leaders. Bruce volunteered to be the advisory coordinator for his high school when the school took up an advisor/advisee program in an effort to "personalize learning" for every student. Two years later, he was finally able to recognize a shift in his colleagues' patterns with him and his principal, a shift that signaled to him that he was leading:

> Over the last month or so, I've noticed that more and more of the staff are approaching me regarding advisory. Some of the new staff have some of the same questions we all had when this program started. Others have ideas that they want to try out and are asking me if it fits under the "parameters" of the program. A couple of teachers have asked if advisory can be used as a conduit for lessons. . . .
>
> I guess the bottom line is that more and more the staff is coming to me first, instead of [the principal's] office. I've spoken to Stan (my principal) as to whether staff are approaching him first with him guiding them off to me. But he has said that no one has approached him regarding advisory issues for quite some time now. In turn, I've turned to Stan less and less as to what my parameters are as advisory coordinator. It seems like I've finally started to truly hold the position as advisory coordinator and that the staff has accepted the transition as well. I obviously still have some things to work on (don't we all?), but it feels nice to have this school leadership that everyone recognizes.

Although he has not directly approached colleagues for feedback, Bruce is noting the shifting behavior patterns between himself and colleagues and these are confirmed by the principal. His leadership of the advisor/advisee program here is clearly focused on students; he is gaining his "leader legs" and that is making him more directly influential in what advisory time is used for. While he has no evidence of the impacts of his leadership work on students, it engages him with colleagues in making good instructional use of their advisory time with students.

We require leader-learners in our programs to obtain feedback from their school colleagues. It can be structured to assess their success at goals in their individual leadership development plans, at grander rubrics for school leadership such as the Interstate School Licensure Consortium standards, or both. Walt, a high school department chair and aspiring principal, elicited written feedback from his social studies department colleagues and administrators. Here are some examples:

> You always take the time to speak with people and to show care and concern for others.

No one more than you believes in the educability of all. . . . Your clearly defined core beliefs are reflected in your work and life.

I have found your willingness to meet with me and discuss issues very helpful. . . . You are an approachable person and I have found your advice worthwhile.

You offer an objective view of a situation that gives perspective needed to see the fairness of a matter.

You have praised my efforts as a teacher, which has given me the confidence to continue trusting my instincts.

From remarks like these, Walt could piece together "how I'm coming across to others." He could also begin to ferret out how his work with his colleagues was helping them, in turn, to work in more effective ways with their students.

Feedback can come, as well, through a structured instrument, such as the Leadership Practices Inventory (LPI), which provides "360-degree feedback" from colleagues (Kouzes & Posner, 2007). For Ted, whom we met in Chapter 2, feedback from the LPI was very influential in shaping his learning goals:

I remember receiving the report back from the Leadership Practices Inventory back in July 2001. The area in which I received the lowest rating was "Encouraging the Heart." This is defined in the participant's workbook as follows:

Accomplishing extraordinary things in organizations is hard work. To keep hope and determination alive, leaders recognize contributions that individuals make. In every winning team, the members need to share in the rewards of their efforts, so leaders celebrate accomplishments. They make people feel like heroes.

I was saddened to feel my colleagues rated me lowest in this area. The very people I was hoping would "march with me" toward school improvement were suffering from "recognition and appreciation deficit disorder." MSLN [Maine School Leadership Network] forces you to take a long and hard look at yourself and ask, "What are my strengths? And what are the areas in which I need serious improvement?" MSLN teaches me that you must be open to that criticism, and you must act to bring about improvement.

Tracing a trail from leader activities to student benefits is considerably more difficult than obtaining feedback. The causal links between what one is trying to make happen for kids and what actually happens for them are complicated. As Chapter 7 will reveal, the 2–3 year timespan of our program often proved too short to yield "documentable evidence" of their impacts on students. But participants could document whether teachers' practices had changed; how staff attitudes supported an improvement; and most valuably, specific cases where teachers were beginning to document impacts on students.

Several things (described in more detail later) made this focus on student performance a productive way to learn about one's own leadership performance:

1. The use of a learning plan (the leadership development plan, or LDP) that situated learning goals in a real leadership arena with specified student learning outcome goals. As in Lori's case with math instruction, this gave participants a set of concrete classroom practices and hoped-for learning gains to document.
2. The availability of diagnostic and assessment tools for student learning. As in Jeanne's case with the personalizing of science instruction, participants often made assessment a part of their strategy for mobilizing staff. The results-based mood of the times helped make collaborative data-gathering and data-based decision-making a source of evidence for examining the success of leadership as well.
3. Support and encouragement from program colleagues and staff, along with our insistence on using performance data, helped to soften the personal risk. As Ted's case illustrates, it takes a good deal of courage to face the prospect that your approach to your work as principal may not be making much difference in kids' learning. Supports in the program and from the workplace had important impacts on leaders' ability to assess their own effects.

Knowing whether one is leading is not easy. Yet paying close attention to their impacts keeps leaders focused on whom they are trying to lead and on what they are leading for. The winds will, as Jeanne said, "come from [the other] direction" once you set your course as a leader. Learning to lead does require courage. As Isabel counseled, "Be intrepid. . . . Take a risk!"

Designers of preparation programs for teachers and leaders have sought increasingly to bridge the "theory-to-practice" gap, recognizing that conventional campus-based methods limit learning to cognitive modes (Norris,

Barnett, Basom, & Yerkes, 2002; Spillane, 2006). The Harvard Graduate School of Education, for example, has developed a sophisticated set of cases from which leadership students can presumably learn leadership and organizational skills. Our experience, however, argues for taking the learner to where the learning is: in the *performance* of real leadership, in real schools, immersed in the relationships that make or break leadership. Even programs that teach skills and situational decision-making fall short. As Jim Spillane put it, "Improved leadership practice does not necessarily follow from improved knowledge and skills, because leadership practice and the actions of individual leaders are not one in the same" (2006, p. 99).

Educators intent on stretching their leadership wings will only know if their wings are stretching by practice, by seeing that "hey, this is about me," and by seeking feedback and evidence of impact on students. Performance alone generates the interpersonal realities that help us know if we can grow and sustain productive relationships with our colleagues. Performance tells us best whether our cognitive grasp of educational matters is sufficient for the task at hand. And only in performance can we encounter ourselves authentically as leaders and thus pursue the intrapersonal journey toward rewiring ourselves to be the best leaders for our schools that we can be.

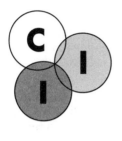

A Pebble in Your Shoe: Where Learning Starts

SIX EDUCATORS HUDDLED AROUND a table at the Senator Motor Inn in Augusta, Maine, pondering Roland Barth's invitation to identify what made their learning "go off the charts." They were teacher leaders and principals participating in the final day of the 2-year Maine School Leadership Network (MSLN) experience.

This small group's list of "necessary conditions" for their learning already counted "the safety to take risks," "integration with my work at school," and "reflection." Someone mentioned "persistence" and another added, "Yes, persistence is important to me the way a pebble in my shoe is: MSLN has helped me to find an important leadership skill I need and to stay with it until I've learned that skill."

Others jumped on this idea and extended it. "Yes, without a program like this, it's too easy to get swept up by the job and never concentrate on getting better at it." "I agree, but for me it took a long time just to figure out which pebble to work on; there were so many and I didn't even know what to call them." "Just like a pebble in your shoe, working on my Leadership Development Plan wasn't comfortable. I had to look hard at myself and say, Hey, you really need to work on this if you want to be a great principal."

Inevitably, it seemed, the group landed on the metaphor of the grain of sand in an oyster that, over time, becomes a pearl. For several of these leaders, the experience of learning to lead felt like persevering despite the pebbles in their shoes, until one became a pearl (or at least, somewhat pearllike).

Many preparation programs for school leaders start in a very different place from what the pebble metaphor suggests. They do not start with the learner so much as they start with a curriculum that lays out a prescription for good leadership. They don't start with the premise that leadership capacity grows in and around that learner so much as they start with the belief that a prescribed collection of knowledge must be acquired by the future leader. They don't start with the notion that leadership grows from tackling challenges in each leader's performance and keeping those uncomfortable pebbles in the center of the developmental process; they start with the premise that some will "get it" and others will not.

The six seasoned leader-learners who lit on the pebble-to-pearl metaphor in May 2004 were confirming the power of learning from personal-professional challenges. The leader-learning literature has documented the power of problem-based learning (Boyatzis, Cowen, & Kolb, 1995; Bridges & Hallinger, 1997; Osterman, 1998), but most programs structure such learning around simulated cases and challenges faced by leaders in general. It was vital for our Maine leaders that their challenges were authentic; they emerged from their own attempts to lead the real people in the schools where they worked. In this chapter, I describe how the process of identifying these challenges and then creating a plan to learn from them often stimulates extraordinary learning.

FINDING A PEBBLE

Some leaders feel that their shoes are loaded with pebbles! They're all too aware of the challenges facing them, chafing against their best intentions to be the leaders their schools need. For them, it can be a challenge simply to isolate one important pebble and focus learning activities on it. Others, among them many novice principals and teacher leaders, have the uneasy feeling that they've got sand in their sneakers, but can't yet articulate what the key challenges are that are the major irritants in their performance. I know several experienced principals who already walk with pearls in their loafers. It can be quite a challenge for them to come to grips with the pebbles lying among those pearls.

Ursula, a middle-school teacher in her 30s, seemed overwhelmed with the collection of pebbles that kept surfacing through the first year of her learning experience. "I want to be effective," she wrote in July 2003, "and able to stand my ground, generate enthusiasm, be proactive, and change the cycle [of failure for underserved students]." She goes on to ponder:

> For those who put up walls, shut down on kids, will I know how to use my power and authority [as an administrator] to enforce and incorporate my philosophy? Will I be too easy, too cooperative, too patient? Will I be able to communicate my philosophy collaboratively, and in a timely manner? Will I think of ways to help motivate teachers to learn? Do I have the cognitive, intrapersonal, and interpersonal tools to enact my purposes?

Ursula is a member of a middle-level teaching team. Although she doesn't have a formal leadership role on the team, she clearly does not shrink from taking on responsibilities. Her informal leadership and her relative youth present myriad challenges. But she eventually centers on one important pebble to frame her learning:

> I believe I will have a difficult time managing and expressing frustration, anger, and disappointment with others . . . At this time I work persistently with others through collaborative efforts. . . . The team I am presently on is still working toward and patiently trying concepts that I have lobbied for, for nearly 3 years. There are times I am angry [and] disappointed, and [when I am] unable to communicate these feelings to [two team members] who are not holding [to their responsibilities in our improvement effort].

Ursula ran across a book about children of alcoholic parents. Reading it, she found that "many of my behaviors and perceptions may be the direct result of being the oldest daughter [in such a family]. My compliance, cooperation, and people-pleasing are the result of trying to adapt and control an uncontrollable environment for 18 years. According to Robert Ackerman [author of the book], one lesson learned was that 'expressing anger was not appropriate' and 'to be acceptable, everything must be perfect.'"

Ursula's pebble, during her yearlong learning-in-practice experience, revolved around this discovery about herself and its implications for her emergence as a leader on her team. She set a learning goal of "actively interacting with others even when it may be conflict." A year later, she wrote of this interpersonal and intrapersonal learning:

> I have been able to address controversies with [a difficult colleague], and voice my disagreement. I so often play or practice things in my head beforehand. It felt nice to see that I can pursue

some of my own needs and for the betterment of our team [by directly addressing issues that stymie us]. Next time, I will try to incorporate a little more breathing while I am working it through.

Ursula's developmental path began with a pebble that was interpersonal, led to intrapersonal exploration, then returned to shaping new interpersonal skills for her to use with her colleague. Her learning journey, in this respect, was very typical of others'.

Hilton, a high school department chairperson, found his pebble in quite a different way. Hilton believed "passionately in standards-based learning and assessment." Articulate and persuasive by nature, he actively lobbied the principal, like-minded teachers, and participants in several politically charged forums. But the principal "dragged his feet," telling Hilton that the faculty needed more information and more time to warm to the idea. Eventually, the principal decided to support standards-based practices and Hilton was "so happy that we are finally going to go in this direction."

The revelation then hit him that "the real work" had not yet started. And here is where Hilton found his leadership pebble:

> Once you've gotten formal support for a change, the real work begins. How to guide the group to understand that our resources must now be spent supporting this move without simply [overwhelming them with] my fervor? It's difficult. . . . The challenge of being a nonadministrator leader has been daunting. I've had to harass, persuade, and lead by example, because edicts were not available to me. I'm not complaining—all of this groundwork has improved the chances of this reform's success manifold.

Hilton's leadership development plan zeroed in on how his actions affected the interpersonal and political dynamics of the faculty group. Recognizing not only that he had little formal power but also that his passion could turn others against standards-based practices, he had to throttle down his overt advocacy and develop a manner with colleagues that took into account what they were thinking and how they were feeling. Leadership success wasn't as clearcut as pursuing his "mission, [the] pathway of reform that I believe—in my heart of hearts—will improve achievement for all students." He was going to learn a great deal more about the interpersonal dynamics of the faculty group and how he could function within it for maximum effect.

Ursula and Hilton found pebbles largely by listening to themselves—to their ruminations about persistent problems in their leadership work, to their feelings of frustration, to the worries that kept them up at night. Their pebbles represent ongoing hurdles between them and their ideals for, in Ursula's case, the students on her midlevel team and, in Hilton's, the success of the district's instructional program. Reflection and conversation with program colleagues and staff helped both leaders sort through many possible pebbles and find one that held possibilities for their own leadership performance.

THE NATURE OF PEBBLES

Ursula's and Hilton's pebbles are unique to them and representative of some broad categories of leadership challenge that surfaced for many leaders in Maine. The range of these is remarkable:

- Creating true investment in new assessment and teaching practices among a teacher team
- Improving the professional norms and culture among a faculty
- Confronting a person in formal leadership regarding the impacts of her or his actions on a faculty or student group
- Engaging grade-level teachers in an examination of their effectiveness with math instruction
- Addressing conflict directly and constructively when it surfaces in faculty meetings
- Providing substantive and legally correct feedback on practice to an underperforming employee
- Speaking comfortably, clearly, and persuasively to a variety of audiences

What makes a pebble in your leadership shoe a promising source of learning? In all likelihood, any pebble can be a productive source of learning if it can be approached with learning in mind. Two qualities, however, seem to make a pebble particularly conducive to learning:

1. It is sufficiently irritating. That is, it's important to success and won't go away; and
2. It sufficiently promises significant personal growth.

If a challenge presents itself frequently in the leader's work, it's persistent enough to be irritating. It causes worry; the leader takes it home with him or her; it becomes a source of self-doubt. Such challenges have risen to a level where they're undercutting the leader's sense of efficacy. It's time to confront and learn from them.

Pebbles have a second quality: the promise of growth. If the challenge is one that falls within the leader's control enough to give him or her the sense that "I can make a change here," it shows the potential for increasing that sense of efficacy. Often, we feel that our greatest challenges are insurmountable. One of the greatest values of a leadership development program and a cohort of fellow leader-learners is that this environment can alter that feeling.

We find that different leaders often identify different pebbles (although some occur more commonly than others). This results from variations in leaders' roles at school; in the cast of characters they work with; and in their own personalities, knowledge base, and readiness. Some leaders come with pretty tough soles so they don't feel some pebbles. Others have very sensitive soles and can easily feel overwhelmed by what feels like a shoeful of pebbles.

Goleman, Boyatzis, and McKee (2002) argue that our emotional and social intelligence, our self-awareness and our awareness of and ease with others, play an important role here. Certainly, our experience bears this out. We as program staff make the identification of pebbles a primary focus of learning activities, particularly in the early phases of our programs. We're looking for pebbles that hold a promise of turning into pearls. We help those whose sneakers are full of pebbles to locate one or two that aren't so irritating that they're overwhelming. For those who just can't feel the pebble or who aren't aware of the irritation, we structure ways to diagnose what's most challenging for the school in its mission for children. And from there, we help to frame what the leader's role is in addressing that challenge and what pebbles, cognitively, interpersonally, and intrapersonally, she or he might find when taking up that role. And, as Hilton's example illustrates, we insist that the pebble serve as the inspiration for a leadership development plan that will guide each leader's learning forward.

COMMON LEADERSHIP CHALLENGES THROUGH THE I-C-I LENS

The I-C-I model of leadership knowledge offers a useful way to understand leadership challenges. It suggests that persistent hurdles to leader effectiveness are the result, in part, of gaps in leaders' interpersonal, intrapersonal, and cognitive knowledge sets. Thinking diagnostically, leaders can more fully understand where and how they can improve their leadership by assessing how their current knowledge and skills may be hampering their ability to handle certain leadership situations.

Take, for example, the challenge facing Shirley in the scenario posed at the beginning of this book. She's charged by her boss—and the state— with implementing standards-based teaching and assessment practices. And her faculty is resisting, some of them angrily. In the faculty meeting, the source of her leadership challenge couldn't be balder: they're not going to do what she's told them they must do. Her challenge lies, as she puts it to herself, in the question, OK, what do I do now?

Shirley faces a leadership challenge that is very common. It can be summarized as "I recognize that you don't agree, but it's got to be done." Administrators are familiar with it, particularly in the current accountability environment, and many formal teacher leaders, such as department chairs and team leaders, have faced it as well. So, what does this pebble look like through the lens of the I-C-I leadership domains? How can the I-C-I framework serve as a diagnostic tool for Shirley's learning?

First, in the *cognitive* domain, Shirley will ask: Am I knowledgeable about the task I'm asking staff to perform? And how knowledgeable are staff? In Shirley's case, this involves understanding a complex set of standards-based concepts and practices, many of which are new to educators. Until leader and staff know more about what they're expected to accomplish, it's going to be very difficult not to feel challenged, fearful, and at a loss. Shirley's own understanding of assessment, of the standards, and of how they apply across the curriculum and for all her faculty rises into view here. If she is to lead her faculty, what must she know of this cognitive pool of information? And what part of that does she already know?

Second, in the *interpersonal* domain, Shirley will ask: Are our working relationships strong enough to weather my forcing the issue with staff? The likely answer is, With some, it is—but how far does my trust and respect extend with them? And, With others, it is not—and if I go ahead and force the issue, how well will the task be done? And will that help or hurt students? And if I force it, what will be the damage to our working relationship—and to my leadership here? From this sort of assessment, Shirley can begin to pinpoint specific staff and particular interpersonal strategies that she might need to use to approach them productively.

Finally, in the *intrapersonal* domain, Shirley will ask: Can I fashion a role for myself here that will permit me to live with myself as a person and as a professional? This line of inquiry might lead her to wonder, Do I believe that this standards-based system is going to benefit all students? And, If I have to force some staff to do it, am I comfortable wielding power in this way—and with handling the fallout from it? Answers to such questions come hard, but they begin with the asking of the question. A great deal of the learning our leaders experience comes through thinking, reading, writing, discussing, and ultimately testing in practice the possible answers that arise.

Shirley's leadership challenge is three dimensional. It has cognitive, interpersonal, and intrapersonal facets. As Shirley ponders how best to respond to the rising resistance on her faculty, it helps to assess her own capacity in each domain. If this challenge rises to the level of a pebble, her self-assessment will help her identify knowledge areas and skills to develop.

Figure 4.1 illustrates five other common leadership challenges parsed out along the I-C-I domains. These are pebbles that many leaders experience, so they are a common wellspring for leadership development. The first two challenges have strong cognitive and interpersonal components: Leaders are wondering whether their knowledge about educational practices is solid enough to merit "taking on" staff or superiors who are not in favor of those practices. The third challenge revolves around finding the way to better practices and outcomes for children when no clear way readily presents itself (a challenge involving extensive cognitive work but constant attention to the interpersonal and intrapersonal dimensions of the change process). The fourth and fifth challenges are primarily interpersonal ones: poor relationships hamper mobilization in the form of dissension within the staff and faculty (fourth) and divisions within the community (fifth).

The I-C-I framework offers leaders, whether novice or seasoned, a way to acknowledge and understand major performance challenges such as these and to use this understanding to frame their professional learning. It is not easy, however, to do this, particularly in the less familiar—and often less validated—interpersonal and intrapersonal domains. It is even more daunting for principals, who carry the presumption of competence, to engage in this learning (Argyris, 1991; Barth, 2001). Two conditions help in this respect: a protected place to reflect on those aspects of the job that are most challenging, and a structure to make learning planful.

PLANFUL LEARNING

The leadership development programs that the leaders in this book experienced followed some basic principles of adult learning. The most basic one has been the subject of this chapter:

1. Professional learning begins with a question that matters to the learner.

The other three are the following:

FIGURE 4.1. Common Leader Challenges: Starting Places for Learning

THE CHALLENGE	COGNITIVE CHALLENGE	INTERPERSONAL CHALLENGE	INTRAPERSONAL CHALLENGE
"I recognize that you don't agree, but it's got to be done." [Staff resist or are unable to change practice to one that you believe is better.]	Am I knowledgeable about what "it" is? Are staff? What do the data say? The professional literature?	Are our working relationships strong enough to weather my forcing the issue with staff? Which staff are unwilling to change? Which are unable? Which are both?	Do I believe that the new practice is going to benefit students? The school? Can I live with myself if I "force" staff? Can I live with myself if I don't make this change happen?
"Those in charge need to know that this directive is wrong-headed." [You must implement a policy/practice that you and staff believe is not in the best interests of children.]	Do I know enough about the directive to argue successfully that it is "wrong-headed"? What do the data say? The professional literature?	How can I walk the line between advocating for my staff/team and respecting the judgment and position of higher-ups? Can I speak up respectfully and with confidence?	Can I live with myself if I "defy my bosses"? If I don't? Can I survive the political fallout?
"We can see that we're not succeeding with every child, but the path forward is not so clear." [You and others recognize the evidence of failure with students, but are not clear about what needs to be done and how.]	Is the evidence reliable and sufficient? Am I certain about the conclusions it leads to? What new practices will address our needs to improve learning, structures, and culture here?	Are our working relationships strong enough to permit me to be honest with others about our failures? How do I approach staff so that they will accept this challenge?	Do I have the energy, skills, and time to devote to this difficult work? Where will my support come from? What's the downside if I don't take this on—for me, for the school, for the kids?
"We must not allow our differences to interfere with our ability as a staff to do the best by our students at all times." [Divisions within staff and professional culture undercut improvement of practice.]	Do I understand why and how staff differ with one another? What concepts and models can help us collaborate on what is best for our students?	How can I convey respect, appreciation, and trust to all staff? How can I reinforce these qualities in staff norms while asserting the need to change? Am I an effective facilitator, mediator, negotiator?	Do I have the patience and skills to compromise, negotiate, reach consensus? Can I speak openly about difficult interpersonal topics? Can I function when emotions are high?
"But the community will not support the work we need to do!" [The community is divided/opposed to initiatives and resources we need.]	What do parents, taxpayers, and others want for our school? Why? How do these square with staff's vision/goals?	How can I and we cultivate respectful relationships and honest dialogue about our school's work? How do we include dissenters? Build consensus?	Am I comfortable with politics? Do I have the energy and skills to lead the community as well as the school?

2. Professional learning is planful.
3. Professional learning is self-directed.
4. Professional learning is reflective and benefits from collegial inquiry and support.

These principles are supported by theory and a growing body of research on learning, adult learning, and experiential learning (see Chapter 9). In this section I take up the second principle; the remaining two are described in more detail in Chapters 8–10.

Having a plan for learning, we have found, has several benefits. Learning from experience—learning in action—is often terribly confusing. The world of leadership, with its swirl of people, ideas, and emotions, is dynamic, multifaceted, and uncertain. It's hard to find a focus, much less stay with it to deepen knowledge or skills. A plan to learn helps learners maintain a focus on their own improvement in the midst of this swirl. When that plan is tied to a specific leadership task in the school, the impacts of that learning can be regularly assessed. And when the plan is shared with helpful colleagues, they can assist in the learning process. The plan and its learning goals are a constant in an often unplanful world where the learning itself emerges from episodes and incidents of practice. Those involved in other leadership development and adult learning programs have found that learning plans have similar benefits (Boyatzis et al., 1995; Mezirow, 2000; Osterman & Kottkamp, 1993).

The system for planful learning we developed, the Leadership Development Plan (LDP), appears in leaders' stories throughout this book. The LDP is a tool to establish some useful learning goals and to frame a manageable number of learning steps designed to help the learner reach those goals. Importantly, the learning goals emerge from a hard look at specific challenges faced by leaders.

The LDP grows from a variety of assessment activities that often include the following:

• An organizational assessment of the leader's school, including the identification of student learning needs; a population of students with those needs; and a diagnosis of the structural, political, and interpersonal staff environment impinging on leadership opportunities (known as an Organizational Profile or School Assessment Profile)
• Identification of a "plan to lead": a goal to improve student learning in the school based on the organizational assessment and some short-term "action objectives" for the leader

- A personal assessment by the leader of her or his:

  > history and position in the school;
  > learning/leadership style and skill set (intrapersonal);
  > values and beliefs regarding the "action" tasks/goals in the
  >   school;
  > relationships with colleagues in the context of the working
  >   relationships among colleagues (interpersonal);
  > knowledge base regarding the "action" tasks/goals in the
  >   school (cognitive).

As the examples of Ursula, Hilton, and Shirley illustrate, leaders use this assessment to turn their attention to their learning (often a very difficult transition, since at this point, most feel that they've done the hard work of identifying the leadership that's necessary and they're raring to get at it!). The LDP asks them to frame their learning around their specific needs in the I-C-I domains and to set goals and identify learning steps to guide the effort to improve performance. The planning sequence is summarized in the following five steps:

1. What is a major challenge *for you* as you move into this leadership activity? (What are your action goals and what's getting in the way?)
2. What aspects of this challenge involve your cognitive knowledge? Your interpersonal knowledge? Your intrapersonal knowledge? (Diagnose current knowledge, skills, dispositions.)
3. State some learning goals in these domains that address your learning needs. (Goal setting.)
4. Establish some learning steps for yourself to enhance your performance in these goal areas. (An agenda for learning.)
5. Often in conjunction with number 4, try out new knowledge, skills, and dispositions in your work and evaluate their effectiveness. (In-action learning and reflection.)

Figure 4.1 illustrates the first two steps in this process. Leaders begin by identifying in specific I-C-I terms the challenges standing between them and their ideals. Step 3, with hints of steps 4 and 5, is illustrated in the following LDP written by Eddie, a first-year assistant principal:

The challenge. How do I work with veteran math teachers in the high school and middle school whose standards for math performance are too low?

Interpersonal action goal. I need to convince teachers that if you expect more, then students will achieve more.

A learning goal (interpersonal). I need to learn to be patient and foster a collaborative process to take place. This will be hard because my natural tendency is to be an adversarial leader and not a democratic one. The learning goal is then to learn how to implement collaborative process techniques while implementing the four specific skills from the cognitive column.

Cognitive action goal. Be more knowledgeable about what makes teachers effective or ineffective and what are effective ways of helping teachers improve.

A learning goal (cognitive). Read *The Skillful Leader: Confronting Mediocre Teaching* [Pratt, Tripp, & Ogden, 2000]. Understand the four specific skills for working with teachers.

Intrapersonal action goal. I need to find the value in the democratic leadership process.

A learning goal (intrapersonal). How do I work within a system where I am in charge and people are reluctant to listen without acting like a [top-down] authority? I must therefore recognize when I am losing faith in the "democratic leadership process" and analyze exactly why. In particular, I foresee me becoming impatient with [four specific teachers] for their negativity and their instantaneous refusal to do something different when it is first introduced.

LDPs are written out and serve as guides (and goads) to keep our colleagues centered in their learning work. We and they have been constantly reminded of the importance of such a plan. The work of educators is filled with "people needs," is immediate, and is demanding. For administrators and for teacher leaders, daily life is full of diverse assignments and can be so nonstop that one's own learning fades by comparison. Having a written plan—and colleagues and staff in our programs who know what it is—protects the learning agenda and bolsters the will to pursue it.

LDPs are, however, not written in stone. We ask (and insist!) that participants use their LDPs as benchmarks for reflection and assessment along their journeys. Thus Eddie's September LDP, above, served as the starting point for his leadership work with four teachers in the fall. As he moved into that work, he routinely reflected on both what he was doing and what he was learning. These observations in turn were shared with staff and colleagues in our program, and as they surfaced from those conversations, they suggested new and often more specific learning and action steps to Eddie. These became further details for the LDP, and so it went.

Episodes of leading encroach on the best and most systematic learning plans. Without a system for reflection and thought, as we will see later in this book, the plan for learning is extraordinarily difficult to follow. Without the disposition to go where the learning takes you, plans become too rigid and can obscure rich lessons. As the group of MSLN leaders noted at the beginning of this chapter, it takes support, safety, adaptability, and most of all persistence to identify a promising pebble, then to work it into a pearl to guide performance.

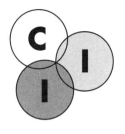

CHAPTER 5

Cultivating Relationships That Mobilize: Interpersonal Learning

In Chapters 1–4, I have introduced the I-C-I framework as a language that has helped leaders understand their professional growth. It has, as well, helped me and my colleagues organize, facilitate, and evaluate our leadership development work. In Chapters 5 and 6, I delve into interpersonal and intrapersonal learning. While I don't intend to underplay the importance of cognitive knowledge to leadership, the nature and value of interpersonal and intrapersonal knowledge has been less understood and less appreciated. For that reason, I devote a chapter to each.

The essential mission of schools, which brim with human connections, is to develop increasingly capable people. This requires intensely interpersonal work with students in the halls, classrooms, offices, and cocurricular venues of schooling. And increasingly, this requires that adults work in intensely interpersonal ways with one another through teaming, collaborative school improvement, and professional learning. Strong leadership engages staff in whole-school matters, promoting thoughtful improvement and "distributing" leadership relationships to all corners of the school and community (Donaldson, 2006; Hargreaves & Fink, 2006; Helgesen, 1995; Meier, 2002; Spillane, 2006; Tschannen-Moran, 2004).

Leaders' paths toward strengthening their schools' performance lie *through others*. Their effectiveness turns on the strength of their working relationships. According to Ronald Riggio (2001):

> Research has consistently shown that leaders who demonstrate consideration behaviors (leaders who are presumably more interpersonally sensitive) lead work groups who are more cohesive, more satisfied, and more productive. . . . Effective leadership is determined by the quality of the interaction between a leader and a particular work group member. (p. 308)

Learning in the interpersonal domain, quite simply, will determine a leader's long-term success and thus the power of her or his school to improve student learning.

As participants in our programs delve into this domain, the floodgates of the relational world open: Shirley's rebellious teachers require a sensitive response; Hilton's fervor for standards-based practices needs to be moderated or he'll drive colleagues away; Ursula must learn the right balance of firmness and understanding to jar her complacent colleagues to action. As one teacher leader put it, "Most of what this [leadership development] is about is interpersonal."

Figure 4.1 presents some common "pebbles" that spur interpersonal learning:

- How to form honest, personally affirming relationships with colleagues, both individually and in groups, "up, down, and sideways" in the hierarchy
- How to shape group norms that guide productive personal and professional behaviors and reinforce collaborative culture both inside the school and between the school and its community
- How to "make" another professional change her or his practice with students
- How to "make" another professional change her or his practice and relationships with fellow educators or parents
- How to "make" those "up the hierarchy" accept information and reasoning they may not be open to

These are not separate interpersonal skills or goals. Leaders usually need to be effective at the first two relationship-building skill sets in order to succeed at the remaining three mobilization skill sets. The essence of their interpersonal work is learning how to mobilize without undercutting relationships. In this chapter I examine a central relational dilemma around which much interpersonal learning revolves and illustrate how Maine educators sought to increase their expertise as relationship-builders and mobilizers.

CAN I—SHOULD I—PUSH?

Experienced leaders in our programs are often all too aware of the tension between "making" staff improve and maintaining strong professional relationships with them. Educators new to leadership are often surprised at the complexity of this tension. But neither veterans nor novices can escape this basic dilemma: How do I push others toward better performance without alienating them?

This dilemma courses through the conversations, the writing, and the LDPs of our participants. It engages them in learning to blend seeming opposites: to facilitate and advocate, to listen and persuade, to be sensitive to others and push. Most find that a deeper dilemma lies beneath this one, a dilemma that is more philosophical and ethical: Should I push? Is it my right to insist on my way? Am I certain enough about what I'm insisting on? This is more an intrapersonal dilemma, as it engages questions of value and belief about a leader's role and relationships. It also has a cognitive element, as it raises questions about the leader's instructional and organizational knowledge bases. These will be taken up in later chapters.

At the root of this interpersonal dilemma often lies the leader's ambition to make a difference for students. For some (especially principals such as Shirley in Chapter 1), the dilemma originates with district policies or initiatives they are expected to carry out. Either way, leaders feel the tug-of-war between their convictions or responsibility and their consideration for others: Do I believe deeply enough to possibly upset the status quo? Am I committed to the level where I can say to others, Hey, we're not doing this well enough and we've got to change? Here looms the great interpersonal bugaboo: conflict. Negotiating the emotions provoked by conflict to fashion consensus and commitment is a common stimulus for interpersonal learning.

In the following example, a seasoned teacher has decided, after much deliberation, that it's worth risking rubbing people the wrong way to raise questions with her elementary school colleagues about "the way we do things around here." Ellen wrote in December, "In my school, those who raised questions about things received flat stares and pat answers [from administrators and veteran teachers]. Such critiques were regarded as a waste of time. The question raisers [like me] complicated and prolonged meetings and received the quiet admonition, Don't make more work for us. I was afraid to ask questions, aware of the general disapproval of upsetting or enlarging the applecart."

In Ellen's Leadership Development Plan, she examined her interactional patterns and pondered how they upset this applecart. The following May, Ellen reflected on her new approach:

> At this point, I was sorely aware of my shortcomings and yet fired up about the way things "could" be around our district. To bolster my courage and resolve, I practiced scripting my thoughts and presentations as part of preparing in a new way for a staff meeting I volunteered to lead, which I hoped would help my coworkers focus on what *they* believed should be happening in our school. As a leader, I hoped to provide a forum in which ideas, complaints, alternatives could be discussed and acted upon in a way that would help us rise above the perpetual grousing, backstabbing, and suspicious nature of our ways.
>
> After quietly enlisting the support of several influential friends, we [engaged the faculty through] a medium-sized circle [process]. I believe that thinking through my own agenda and garnering support before the meeting were essential for the meeting's success. The following day, I wrote a note to members of the organizing team to thank them. These are significant changes in the way I communicate with coworkers and higher-ups.

Ellen's determination to improve her school motivated her to look more closely at the patterns of relationship and interaction and where she fit into them. Her learning plan helped her devise new ways of interacting both outside and inside the faculty meeting setting. Although stepping out from the rank and file is a tremendous risk, one often viewed with "suspicion and fraught with ostracism," as she noted, she felt certain that it is what leaders do.

Many people come to our program confusing administration with leadership; principals and superintendents dominate their images of leaders and how they operate. Too often, these are not productive images because, for many, administrators have been "all push and no relationship." Once introduced to the power of relationships in affecting leaders' success, many, like Tim, become aware that they need to develop their interpersonal capacities if they are to "plow ahead," as Tim puts it, without losing their staff.

> I have a tendency to plow ahead with tasks that I have. . . . I recognize that I run the risk of losing the support of my teachers if they feel that I am ramming my own ideas on them without their

approval. . . . The saying "The road to hell is paved with good intentions" is absolutely true. Regardless of my intentions, I need to be more sensitive and aware of the impact of even the simplest decisions. I can avoid developing tunnel vision by being more reflective about the impact of decisions before making them.

Coming to terms with the "push" dilemma is fundamental to effective leadership in schools. It helps learning leaders understand how they can best influence others, what their authority and power are, and how these can be exercised without alienating others. Principals, like Tim, often seek ways to form and strengthen working relationships despite their power and authority. They learn to engage in what Blasé and Anderson (1995) call "power with" rather than "power of" or "power through." Teacher leaders often come to this quite naturally. In Libby's words,

At first, I was very resistant to the idea that it was appropriate for me to push my colleagues to examine their effectiveness at all [in this evaluation project]. . . . How would people perceive me if I started running around saying, Hey, let's examine *your* practice and see how you can improve! These views came from fear. I didn't know how to push. And even if I did, I was not comfortable doing it [the way principals do it]. I had to learn my own way.

Whether the "push" dilemma involved a colleague; a subordinate; a community member; or as it often did, the superintendent or a board member, our participants benefited from reflection on their own values and priorities and clarifying their beliefs in a written platform (see Chapter 9). But this intrapersonal and cognitive work only set the stage for the important work of learning how better to form relationships that were resilient enough to turn the leader's push into true mobilization for improvement.

MOBILIZATION SKILLS

How do I "make" a colleague change? A range of options surface for the leader intent on learning how to mobilize others: order him to change, cajole her to change, persuade him, collaborate with her, offer incentives. In this section, I share examples of common mobilization skills that our participants chose to work on as they focused their learning around this most central of all leader tasks.

Confronting Avoidance

Jeanne, a high school department chair, sought to reengage Ben, a senior member of her department who had withdrawn from their increasingly important instructional innovation work. She drew from an article to create an interpersonal strategy to try with Ben:

> I used the *How to Confront* suggestions [from a MSLN handout] within the science team [because] it had become painfully obvious that the senior science team member felt separated from the group. His attendance at meetings was sparse, his attention to details even worse. As the science team leader, I became concerned that the current direction of the majority of the team would only serve to completely alienate our senior member, [just when we faced many tasks related to improvement that required us to work as a team].
>
> After recognizing that problems do not go away, they just go under, I read through the *How to Confront* handout. Setting up an appointment and establishing a safe environment were easy. The planning of the discussion and the decision to focus on the issues and not the person was also easy. . . . [Jeanne next describes how the meeting went, concluding with the following.] I asked what could be done to help him "come back" [into the group] and then sat back and listened. . . .
>
> Since then, we have unanimously agreed to study portfolio assessment. We have mapped out our curricula as well as aligned it with the [state learning standards]. We have had five science team meetings regarding assessment and Ben has missed only one. His attendance as well as his attention has made for a much stronger team.

Jeanne continues to focus her own developmental work on these skills: recognizing that problems do not go away; establishing safe environments; focusing others on avoided issues; asking, What can help you?; and listening.

Facing Conflict Authentically

Marilyn is a team leader in a secondary school. By her own description, she was a "fix it" type of administrator, because, as she discovered in her reflections, she "wanted to avoid conflict": "When I wanted to avoid conflict, I'd want to *fix it right off*. That day. I'd respond quickly, I'd be sort of reactionary and fix it all, and like smooth it over and make everything peachy. . . . I'd fix it!" Her breakthrough was understanding "that conflict is not a negative thing, that conflict is a way for me to work with people, to sit down and . . . problem-solve through a situation that's affecting students or affecting staff."

Marilyn's Leadership Development Plans led her toward a new strategy to "name" the problem and "share it back" with those who are feeling conflicted by it. As she said in an interview:

> Now I have confidence to say, "We don't have the answer to this, we don't have the information we need, it's going to take us some time, some time to talk to the stakeholders, to talk to the student, to sit back and take a longer, more reflective, more in-depth investigation of what's going on or why this is happening."

Marilyn's learning included developing new interpersonal strategies that would promote collaborative problem-solving. She explained:

> If we don't listen to other people, we don't really understand them. If we don't understand them, we're not asking the "why" questions. I guess I've trained myself to do that. . . . I reflect when I go back to my office because I've taught myself to do that. . . . It's quiet and I'll go, Oh my, I didn't listen for understanding. And then I'll go back and I'll say, I didn't listen to you carefully. And I've apologized to people and I've been *genuine*. And I'm telling you that's all it takes to make a change.

Although different participants developed different strategies for learning from the conflicts in their leadership work, every participant faced challenges of negotiating the emotions, the interpersonal balkanization, and the politics created by conflict.

Structuring a Positive Setting

Most participants identified learning goals related to facilitation and communication skills. The more they examined their responsibilities, the more they saw that their own comfort and facility in leading groups or intervening with colleagues or parents to mediate differences and to problem-solve are essential to their success.

Many focused on their own capacity to stay attuned to the interpersonal cues in groups they were either facilitating or participating in. Karl, an experienced principal, noted in a reflective journal that he had begun to see growth in his understanding of

> three facilitation skills, namely, controlling physical space by putting tables in a circle, using active listening skills, and providing an opportunity for all the staff members to share comments during two segments of roundtable discussions. As I have either facilitated meetings this year or been an active observer, I have consistently utilized all three of these skills at the meetings.

Teachers who were new to leadership often had a great deal of experience in meetings, but little understanding of how to structure and facilitate an effective one. Veronica volunteered to facilitate two staff groups at her school and used these experiences to examine the interpersonal dynamics of her own facilitation skills. It turned out to be a powerful learning experience: "I learned it's important to be up front with the people you are asking to join you [on a committee]. They must be aware of the time and energy commitment before signing on so you can have members who are truly invested in the project. I have also learned that flexibility is necessary. . . . Frustration and disinterest can prevail and taint the project. Keep it simple."

Program staff and faculty teach and model group facilitation skills in our cohorts and coach small learning teams of participants to learn the process-product balance in their own work. By and large, participants are hungry for these skills and many find it comfortable, having experienced them in program activities, to transfer them to their own leadership work.

Blending Process and Product

Monitoring relationships on an individual basis or within a group setting benefited as well from exposure to intervention skills and templates for using influence productively. Nora, a teaching principal, made this a central part of her learning plan, so she could become a better "on the side" facilitator of meetings:

> I cannot truthfully say that I am the leader of this literacy/language group [consisting of myself,] the speech and language teacher, and the literacy teacher in our building. I can say, however, that I've taken more notice over the past few months of how this group functions. All suggestions are valued during our discussions. We discuss the needs of children as observed by all of us.
> I've been more careful this year to document our planning and observations and I'm looking more closely at the outcomes with

children as they relate to our lessons. Also, I've called attention in group meetings to the way we all work together. In addition to asking how the lesson went, we can check in with each other about the effectiveness of our planning sessions.

Intervention

Another common interpersonal skill is intervening to improve working relationships that have gone sour. Stan, a principal, struggled to intervene productively with an overbearing staff member whose relationships with other staff were undercutting the success of a program he was running. Stan's efforts to learn to use intervention skills finally began to bear fruit:

> I am also exhibiting "growth" in "collaborating with staff as challenges arise." For example, I organized a meeting between a "challenging colleague" and the guidance counselor. . . . I needed the guidance counselor to work with us to create an effective program [but the challenging colleague was making him feel unwelcome]. . . . I wanted the challenging colleague to change her "language of complaining" to a "language of commitment" (*How the Way We Talk Can Change the Way We Work: Seven Languages for Transformation*, by Kegan and Lahey [2001]) [so the two could collaborate as they needed to].
>   . . . . [The meeting started out OK, but then there were several fiery interchanges between the two]. . . . I had to step in. I told the guidance counselor that he had to let [the challenging colleague] finish talking. I told the guidance counselor he had to give her the same respect she was now giving him. Later on, he felt I was reprimanding him and siding with her. I explained I thought he was not providing her with the same respect as he had expected.
>   This was a safe intervention for me as a leader. I felt strongly in my observation of the situation and my decision to intervene. I did not feel threatened by the individual and I responded in a respectful, but blunt, manner ("Please let her finish"). This is the key—I was not "threatened" by the guidance counselor. What characteristics threaten me? This is an area I need to explore.

These examples of mobilization skill development demonstrate how learners tried to enact new interpersonal strategies—new behavior sequences—to induce others to improve their work with students. Central to this core knowledge area are skills that, as Fullan (2003) puts it, "face problems" that encumber school improvement, rather than avoid or suppress them. These are skill sets for facilitating clear communication, expressing feelings, problem finding, problem solving, consensus, and collaborative action.

Our participants, as Jeanne and Stan illustrate, often found that articles and books helped them to conceptualize new strategies to use. Works dealing with conflict, with how to work with difficult colleagues, with group facilitation and group dynamics, and with action planning are excellent resources (see List of Resources). In this fashion, cognitive learning presented relevant ideas and techniques that could be integrated into Leadership Development Plans as models and strategies for interpersonal performance. Specific behavioral sequences keyed to specific situations such as a colleague's request of Marilyn to fix a problem he was having with another colleague could then be activated when the occasion arose.

Making smart decisions about mobilization also benefits from *organizational analysis skills*. These help leaders read cues on an institutional scale, focusing on relationships among others and the climate and politics of the school and community in general: Are we ready to take on this serious new effort to address these learning needs? Who is ready and who is not? What intergroup dynamics—political or personal—will be activated? What does all this mean for me as I begin this important leadership venture? We think of these considerations as requiring *organizational literacy*—one of the two core knowledge areas in the cognitive domain.

For many teachers just beginning to consider leadership, the discovery of organizational dynamics is an eye-opener. We routinely use, for example, Bolman and Deal's *Reframing Organizations* (2005) in our cohort program. It not only provides a variety of lenses to use in examining what's happening in school, it also offers leaders a way to understand their own tendencies toward one frame or the other and their blind spots when it comes to organizational cues. Similarly, tools that identify different learning or interaction styles, such as the Myers-Briggs Type Inventory (Myers-Briggs Foundation, 2006) or Kolb's Learning Style Inventory (1999), give learners a vocabulary for understanding others' and their own behaviors and feelings in mobilization work.

RELATIONSHIP-BUILDING SKILLS

Bruce, a high school teacher leader, wrote that his learning plan helped "me get beyond seeing everything as political so I can see and hear the value that people I might disagree with bring to the [discussion] and keep them constructively involved in the advisor/advisee program." Bruce's remark crystallizes the importance of relationships to leadership. If leaders don't "see and hear the value that people . . . bring to the discussion," those people will not feel valued. There's a good chance that they will not be fully engaged in the leader's mobilization efforts. Learning to operate in a trusting, open manner with colleagues and fostering those relationships among them unlocks the capacity to act.

The second core interpersonal knowledge area, relationship building, revolves around leaders' understanding of their own relationships with others: Is our relationship strong enough to accommodate my being honest about my views of what needs to happen here? Are they resilient enough to withstand—or even better, benefit from—conflict? The most powerful lessons for many leaders grew from learning to monitor interpersonal cues in their own interactions, to watch and listen intently, and to interact in a manner that cultivates honest working relationships.

Christopher, a technology coordinator, sought to engage "fringe people" in implementing computer-based instructional techniques. He found that he needed first to connect with these people as people and professionals, a process that required him to set aside his goals for them for the moment:

> As part of my [Leadership Development Plan], I focused on depersonalizing issues and really focusing on discussions with the fringe parties that might be affected by changes but were not represented on the committee. . . . All of these personal actions have had benefits. . . . I believe it centers on building of trusting relationships. To promote this trust building, I have practiced really listening, consciously, to the point of becoming habit, to people all along the way. I have altered my listening skills and body posture to augment this end. Specifically, focusing on eye contact, standing face to face with a person, sometimes lowering my stature in relation to them, paraphrasing to check for understanding and finally following up repeatedly.
>
> I view each interaction with anyone as an opportunity to build trust, honest trust, that sometimes leads to disagreement, but still respect and understanding of each other's position or reason. And that, in turn, helps foster ongoing relationships.

The following are relationship-building skills that many participants sought to develop.

Making Communication with Peers Honest and Respectful

School leaders succeed through optimizing participation in deliberations and decisions. Many of our colleagues practiced a variety of listening and collaboration skills in their effort to learn how to keep channels open and not shut others down. Here, Lori writes about her progress in using "straight talk":

> I began to revisit the use of straight talk [in the 2nd year]. Prior to and following the Deborah Tannen article, "That's Not What I Meant" [1998], I gained new insights into the uses and abuses of straight talk. I had used it in the past with colleagues, thinking I was just being honest, when really I may have left people feeling belittled or humiliated. If my goal was to create an ally who could see my sincere point of view, I had to figure out how to use straight talk to my benefit. One simple step really made all the difference in the way my straight talk was received. Before using it, I began by asking permission. Below are examples of my more meaningful straight talk exchanges.

Many of Lori's and Christopher's program colleagues addressed similar skills: listening with their ears, eyes, and bodies; setting aside their own solutions and judgments for a time; asking questions and making assessments rather than making statements and assertions; checking for understanding; and asking permission to offer advice and feedback.

Making Communication Up the Hierarchy Honest and Respectful

Many participants face the challenge of pushing back when they believe, as Shirley's faculty did, that requirements and initiatives are counterproductive. Their interpersonal learning revolves around how to talk "up the hierarchy" in a productive way. Here, Molly, a teacher leader, summarizes in an e-mail to her Maine School Leadership Network learning team a "quick success" in her effort to practice talking "assertively, yet respectfully" to her principal:

> Hi all,
>
> Just wanted to share a quick success I had yesterday with my principal. Have really been working on being more open and honest (assertive) these days. Well, was in a meeting with [the principal] the other day and a comment she made was really disturbing to me. I sat on it overnight and the next day went to meet with her. She was unavailable so I emailed her with all of the "I" language. I was very honest about my feelings and how I felt I was treated by her. Well, to my surprise, she came right up to me and apologized! I was shocked. It lead to a good conversation about my feelings and how I think she speaks to me sometimes. For me— it was great success! Small steps!

Especially for teacher leaders, relationship building with administrators through authentic, respectful interactions ensures the inclusion of teachers' opinions in school decisions and provides an antidote to the divisiveness that can grow between staff and administration.

Honoring Differences of Opinion

Leaders can lead only as far as their colleagues are willing to go. If individuals or groups are not convinced of the merits of the leader's methods or goals, leaders need to give time and effort to accommodating these views and values. Lena, an experienced elementary teacher, came to this realization:

> I'm just beginning to learn how to have a relationship with someone [where it's OK with them and with me that] they don't have to like all my decisions. . . . [I'm] beginning to understand how relationships cycle . . . that I need not fear conflict . . . and beginning to understand the importance of my own actions in relationships.

Lena's Leadership Development Plan focused on her being more patient and less "impetuous" in pushing her viewpoint:

> I'm working on talking less, listening more; not to "take up too much space in the room" or to be "too forceful." . . . I am learning what is important to others and more about my beliefs and triggers. I also realize and recognize other people's strengths and skills [as I] look at our staff development needs through a "relationship" lens rather than a "what needs to be fixed" lens. [This] has allowed me to see needs more clearly . . . and to have hope.

Lena is developing a new perspective on the part she plays in the interpersonal mix and how it shapes her learning goals for improving her participation. Besides working on important interpersonal skills, she's engaged in checking the intrapersonal habit of forming opinions prematurely about where the other person is coming from:

> [What was very powerful learning for me was learning to look at my] assumptions about other people's behavior. "They are doing this because of that." . . . Learning to check the assumption and question it . . . gave me a better perspective on what other people were thinking. Because so often you do not hear what other people are thinking in a work environment.

Relationship-building skills help leaders clarify the purpose of and values in working together (Donaldson & Sanderson, 1996; DuFour, Eaker, & DuFour, 2005; Garmston & Wellman, 1999). These include monitoring the receptivity of others to them and to their ideas, eliciting discussion and dialogue instead of competition and persuasion, establishing authenticity in the relationship that promotes honest communication and clear roles, and developing ways to determine from colleagues how their leadership efforts are being received. Listening carefully and appreciatively to others' words and intentions became a significant skill set for many of our participants.

Frameworks exploring interpersonal dynamics offer useful descriptions of interactions and techniques that can be incorporated into learning plans. (See, for example, Johnson & Johnson, 1995; Kegan & Lahey, 2001; Tannen, 1995.) Personality- and interaction-style inventories, conflict management inventories, and 360-degree feedback devices help participants assess their own skills and dispositions. We often incorporated into program sessions "trainings" in relational skills such as conflict resolution or soliciting feedback, followed by opportunities to practice new techniques in role-play situations.

INTERPERSONAL LEARNING HAPPENS INTERPERSONALLY

In summary, productive interpersonal learning focuses on five layered skills sets that can be organized as follows:

1. Deepening my comfort and skill at forming solid working relationships with a variety of people—*an endeavor that leads to* . . .
2. Monitoring others and situational cues: listening; diagnosing needs; using organizational, group, and interpersonal frameworks and social and emotional awareness to discern what people and the school need from you—*an endeavor that leads to* . . .
3. Intervening with others to mobilize: facilitating coming together; problem-solving; delegating; spearheading action; negotiating between authority/power and consensus; drawing in cognitive frameworks about teaching, learning, and school improvement—*and* . . .
4. Monitoring the health and sustainability of individual and group relationships in action; *and throughout* . . .
5. Monitoring yourself and how you're doing

The leaders in this chapter point to a basic and frustrating truth about gaining these skills and dispositions: Because relationships are ebbing and flowing, learning how to behave differently *among them* is a fleeting process. A leader can't say, in the middle of a meeting, "Wait, let's back the tape up and let me try another strategy." As I note in Chapter 9, interpersonal learning requires heavy doses of social and emotional awareness, reflection, and feedback from colleagues. Of the three dimensions, interpersonal learning most needs to take place in real time and with real people. As Lave and Wenger (1991) put it, this learning is heavily "situated" in the relational realities of our workplaces; it simply cannot occur fully outside the leadership situation itself.

Learning "in performance" requires cultivating an observer's eye to watch how you perform. Olivia, an elementary principal, described this process of "performance learning" as follows:

> I've been working on my "response-ability," the ability to choose my response to people and events rather than simply react [which sometimes makes matters worse when I am faced with conflict]. I try to keep in mind Eleanor Roosevelt's saying "No one can hurt you without your consent." I cannot adequately communicate how this one phrase has affected my life this year. In spite of my outgoing personality, I am an introvert. I need time to process internally, to rehearse responses, to converse in private before participating in public conversations. . . . I often feel that I respond most effectively after the encounter [in a conflict situation] when I have had the chance to process the conflict and my response to it.
>
> It is one of those times when I have looked in the mirror and seen a new potential in my face. Taking a proactive stance has made a difference in several relationships this year, particularly in my work with the school committee.

Here is the intimate relationship between action and learning that typifies the interpersonal domain. Without "real time" effort to make something happen within a discernible arena of school life—with "real people" and a "real agenda"—it would be impossible for our participants to "see and feel" that their efforts to change how they interrelate with others have born fruit.

Organizing journal entries, critical event analyses, feedback, and reflective narratives can help bring structure to the process of interpersonal reflection that is so essential to learning from interpersonal experience. (See Chapters 7 and 8.) Interactions are difficult to write about; they occur in nanoseconds and are gone. Emotions and unspoken motives often course through them, and there's too little time to reflect on their effects before they've disappeared. We, as staff, seek ways to help participants not only document what worked and why but to plan to repeat what worked so that these lessons become part of their repertoires. This seems to be a critical departure point in performance learning: how to capture what works and practice it again at the appropriate moment so that it sticks.

Goleman and colleagues (2002) draw from recent brain research to show that mood and emotion dynamically shape the relationships that grow up among leaders and colleagues. "Mood impacts results," they say (p. 12), and leaders' interpersonal awareness and self-management are thus essential to making an interchange with another person or group work out for the best. Lewis, Amini, and Lannon's wonderful book, *A General Theory of Love*, explains how our limbic systems allow "feelings [to be] contagious, while [thoughts] are not" (2000, p. 64). Our emotions flow back and forth in "open loops" within the group or conversation. We cannot join others in a faculty meeting or team planning sessions without registering and influencing their feelings, attitudes, and commitment.

So the interpersonal domain engages emotional communication as much as—and often more than—cognitive communication. Goleman and his colleagues note that reaching intellectual consensus in a work group often requires attaining "emotional resonance" as well (2002). Failure in the "low road" of emotions and relationships often means failure on the "high road" of thoughts and plans (Goleman, 2006). "The emotional art of leadership," write Goleman et al., "includes pressing the reality of work demands without unduly upsetting people [and seeing your goals suffer an] emotional highjacking" (2002, p. 13).

For leaders in schools, where proximity and access to colleagues is so great and where so much business is transacted face to face, the best-laid plans of leaders often undergo emotional highjackings. So interpersonal learning—the ability to alter old patterns of behaving together—is essential to effective school leadership. Altering patterns of behavior, as brain research increasingly shows, is "best learned through motivation, extended practice, and feedback" (Goleman et al., 2002, p. 102).

Our participants were often intensely motivated to delve into the interpersonal dynamics of their own leadership activities. The I-C-I framework, by simply acknowledging the importance of relationships to leadership, gave them permission to talk about, examine, and explore alternatives to their own interpersonal repertoires. Some found the messiness and emotion of this arena frightening. Others resisted conceding that their power to attain goals depends on mobilizing the will and energy of others. And for some the relational world was simply so foreign that they struggled to learn its language and to see how emotion and affiliation shaped their own leadership success.

But few finish our programs without agreeing with one seasoned principal, who declared, "I've never focused on any kind of interpersonal skills in my career. [In the Maine School Leadership Network] we were learning a lot of communication skills, how to relate to other people and to deal with conflict, how to listen effectively, etc., and I could see that I had made a lot of mistakes as a 'leader' by not listening and by assuming that I was always right."

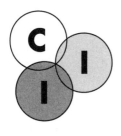

CHAPTER 6

In the Heart of the Learner: Intrapersonal Learning

> Real leadership comes from the quiet nudg-
> ing of an inner voice.
> —Madeleine Albright, University of North
> Carolina Commencement, 2007

OUR COLLEAGUES CARRY ON THEIR OWN conversations with themselves as they learn what it means for them to lead. Learning to lead isn't just about what should happen in school and what others need to do. At its heart, it's "about me and whether I'm fit" for leadership. As they learn how leadership works, many of our colleagues return to two persistent intrapersonal questions: Do I really want to do this? Can I do this well? Jeanne captured these in a midprogram taking-stock reflection when she wrote,

> Challenges in [the intrapersonal domain] are that sometimes I do not want to be a leader; I just want to be a regular person. I want to let my hair down. I do not always want to do what is right, nor do I want to be placed on some kind of leadership pedestal. . . . [As shown by their feedback,] my colleagues seemed to think that I was close to the "walking on water" phase of leadership. I certainly did not place myself there.

Jeanne went on to ponder a fundamental dilemma for leaders:

> I'm not sure I *want* to be a leader if it means I can no longer be
> myself. *Can* I deliver on the promise of leadership? Can I "walk my
> talk"—be the leader I aspire to be, for both my school and myself,
> even if my colleagues believe I can?

The first element of this intrapersonal quest is about leaders' choice
to lead. The learning journey engages educators in exploring what the real
work of leading is about and assaying whether that work is rewarding and
sustaining for them. The second is about leaders' ability to "walk the talk"—
to be the kind of people who spawn in others the spirit of leadership that
mobilizes them to do better things for students and the school. Here, learning to lead is about having "the right stuff," about learning what "stuff" I
have that works. As Ellie put it, it's about

> exploring the blind and hidden aspects of myself [and examining]
> the question, what is leadership and what is my role as a leader?

The intrapersonal domain is where we weigh the choice to be a leader
(Buchanan, 1996). Seeking greater understanding of our own skills, temperament, and interpersonal style, we hope to feel steadily more self-
confident in a leadership niche and to know what that niche is. Isabel
expressed it this way:

> What's reduced the risk [of this journey toward leadership] for me
> is being able to define the kind of leader I want to be. . . . How I
> can fit into the system and how I won't or can't. . . . There's a
> grounding underneath my thinking now, my understanding of the
> kind of leader I can be.

We actively stimulate this intrapersonal journey, for it often leads to a blend
of self-confidence and self-awareness that we find essential in a leader.
This blend, in turn, encourages and guides interpersonal and cognitive
learning and ensures that these leaders will continue to be learners as long
as they lead.
    This chapter contains samples of leaders' intrapersonal learning jour-
neys, focusing on these two strands of that journey: unpacking the will to
lead and exploring whether "I've got what it takes" to deliver on those
ambitions to lead. Curiously, most participants came to our programs not
expecting to encounter the intrapersonal domain so directly. Yet most

found that it lay at the heart of their journey. Here is how Grace described this discovery:

> It wasn't until sometime in February or March [in the first year], when Mary shared some questions that she had happened upon in her reading, that I began to look at who I am, in this role as a teacher leader. I shared these questions [and this] led to what I consider a huge breakthrough:
>
> - Where do I need to grow?
> - What are the encouragers and enhancers to my growth?
> - What is it like, being a teacher leader in my school?
> - What long-term commitment am I going to make to my leadership?
> - Why is this role of teacher leader important to me?
>
> It wasn't until one of our Taking Stock sessions that someone said, "It's all about *you*!" . . . I began to think about what I now consider *my* essential questions [above] and it was because of those that I began to question what it was that people saw in me [as a leader] that I couldn't see in myself. At that point, I changed the focus of my [Leadership Development Plan] . . . to gaining knowledge I thought I needed to know about who I am and who other people think I am [as a leader among them].

Grace's realization that her own success and identity as a leader are tied to "who other people think I am" profoundly captures the intersection of the interpersonal and the intrapersonal. Leadership in schools, after all, isn't simply about what individuals do; it's ultimately about how the collective is mobilized by the dance that leaders stimulate among their colleagues.

WHERE THERE'S A WILL—IS THERE A WAY?

Individuals' will to lead is rooted in their motives as educators and as people. Their belief systems about what schools are for, how children learn, and how adults should behave and think in order to support learning shape how leaders frame their own behaviors and strategies as school leaders. As leaders open themselves to learning and look more closely at their own performance, their motives—their will to lead—are inevitably tested. Giving voice to intrapersonal questions such as Grace's makes them apparent, helping leaders to wrestle with them and, hopefully, come to a clearer understanding of why (and whether) leadership is a sound professional choice for them.

Vicki, a school counselor aspiring to greater leadership, tapped into her motives *and* her temperament:

> The personal quality that will best aid in my learning [as a leader] is my desire to make my school the best school it can be. If I am working on behalf of people I love, I have a fiercely competitive nature. I act in ways that I would never act on my own behalf. For my students, I will master skills I would find too tedious to do in my everyday life.

Vicki's deep commitment to the parents of her elementary school guides her work and relationships. These form a foundation of trust and authenticity, a wellspring of her ambition to lead:

> My acceptance into [this school] is based mainly on my personal relationships with my former students who are now parents of my elementary students here. I now work for them. I am thankful for those relationships, because these people know who and what I am. They know that I will fight tooth and nail for a child I love, long before I would defend myself. They know that I don't put up with misery from kids [and] that I have [high] expectations of kids' behavior.

The passion Vicki feels for students and their families transcends any purely intellectual leadership motives. Hers is a visceral motivation, a deep will to make a difference. After considerable self-observation and reflection, Vicki made a discovery about herself: Good leaders need more than deep passion for their work and their students. As a graduate of the rural high school where she had previously worked, Vicki had a sense of commitment that could easily lead to righteous indignation toward some colleagues, creating a dynamic that, she eventually realized, blocked her ability to lead:

> When I sat in [the high school] faculty meetings, I thought that my vote should count more than others' votes. I was so resentful of teachers "from away" who would drive into town in their little Volvos and say, "Our kids need . . ." All I could think was, What the hell do you know about what our kids need? Why don't you go back to where you came from?

Eventually, I was able to grow past those resentments and see that a fresh perspective could help our school and our kids in the long run. Those of us who were entrenched in the history and politics of the school were often blind to the ways in which [the school] was lacking, simply because we had never seen anything else.

Vicki was outspoken, and particularly when advocating for her students and her school, she could be "fiercely competitive." Her reflective writing eventually revealed a second self-realization, this one related to how she needed to modulate some of her natural tendencies:

I need to show that a woman can make decisions that are as valid as those of a man, but not maintain the sharp edge that I see so many women portray. I feel that this sharp edge is not conducive to building relationships.
. . . By offering a nurturing, caring environment, I realize that I also open myself up to attacks from those who perceive this as a weak stance. . . . [When I continue to be competitive and outspoken,] I need to be ready to be called the *B* word and accept it as a badge of courage. I also need to always remember that it is not a sign of weakness to show compassion and empathy.

Vicki's writing captures the familiar tones of intrapersonal dialogue, of self-realization: "I realize that . . . I need to be ready. . . . I also need to always remember . . ." She, like many learning leaders, is making notes for herself, coaching notes that she hopes to recall when she's in situations where they will be useful. She is becoming more adept at intrapersonal learning. She is finding ways to observe herself, to see more clearly how she operates in leadership situations. And she's gradually building ways to manage herself differently in situations where her natural inclinations to talk, behave, think, and feel are not conducive to productive outcomes.

This learning process helped Vicki find a workable way to express her will to lead. As with all participants in our programs, she came because she was willing to lead—or at least to think of herself as a potential leader. Like others, she had been encouraged by colleagues who had seen in her (and in her outspokenness, her passion, her willingness to speak out) that same potential. Her learning was all about finding a way to match her will.

CAN I LEAD? A MATTER OF VALUES AND CAPABILITY

Matching the will to lead with a way to lead: This is the essence of the intrapersonal learning journey. Vicki's story illustrates the early stages of sorting out whether and how one is suited for leadership. Nora's story illustrates the mature stages of recognizing how a leader's values and capabilities "fit" her or him more to one leader role than to another. Nora was a seasoned and much respected teacher in a small elementary school who was asked to "step up" into a principalship at her school a few years before she joined MSLN. Here, she voices the central question of her "fit" with that role:

Four years ago, when my principal asked me to be the teaching principal for the building, I wondered what qualities he saw in me and, a year later, why he encouraged me to apply for the teaching principal position. . . . It was surely nothing for which I'd studied. Was it something with which I was born, or raised? I think I'm closer to contemplating these questions more seriously [at the halfway point of the MSLN program], but more importantly, understanding my limits and where this knowledge will take me.

In her new administrative role, Nora encountered a number of expectations and demands that she hadn't fully anticipated. She describes having to cut an ed tech position and, later, the stress of evaluating teachers and not recommending a probationary teacher for continuing contract. And this did not sit well with her:

I was in constant internal conflict in making a decision [about which ed tech to cut] and carrying it out, but I knew that this work was going to be mine alone. Whatever the decision, there would be confrontation and conflict, which I wanted to avoid, avoid, avoid. My mode of operation [in the building] became more reactionary, instead of proactive. . . . The idea that these teachers would be so distrusting of my "motives" was hurtful. My penchant for avoidance of confrontation was winning and I avoided them as much as they avoided me. However I *had* made a tough decision, which I hoped was child centered.

Faced with the harsh reality that administrators need to be bosses, Nora grew very concerned about her relationships with her faculty. The stress of this administrative leader role was taking a toll on her personally and, she believed, on her effectiveness as a leader. Most telling, she felt that her new leadership role was compromising her established and fulfilling identity as a great teacher.

I was finding myself exhausted at the end of leading each meeting of the staff. My confidence level, instead of growing, was waning. I felt like I needed a reality check at every turn. How was I being perceived by the majority of the staff? This was a question I wanted to ask them, but was not sure I had the confidence to face the answers and still continue with the rest of the year. . . .

More and more I was beginning to feel that I was ineffective in both of my roles. Perhaps my role as principal was getting in the way of the work I wanted to lead. My role as teacher seemed to be taking a backseat to the principalship and I was feeling inefficient there, too.

In Nora's retrospective portfolio at the end of the MSLN program, she was able to pinpoint a major breakthrough in her intrapersonal learning that eventually changed her leadership work at her school:

One day in March, I'd had it with all of the overload at school dealing with student issues, parents, nitpicky staff, and home responsibilities. I thought, "Where in my work life am I happiest?" The answer blared at me. . . . "In kindergarten!" The classroom is where I'm most happy.

So Nora decided to step down from her principalship to a leadership role more suited to her.

Let the chips fall where they may. I needed to do what was best for me and what is best for me at this time of my life is to get into a classroom and continue to learn and use my craft as a teacher. Teacher leadership will need to take on a new look for me. My journey through the principalship has led me to a major intra-personal discovery: I don't want to be the person who is solely responsible for leading, setting high expectations, demanding adult learning, assessing, identifying, applying, and actively engaging others to care about quality education. I don't want to continue to "herd cats and push rope." . . .

I want to be a part of that leadership, but I don't want to be the driving force in my school. I don't want to be the keeper of the power, a "gift" with which I'm clearly uncomfortable. It's lonely and you get beaten up a lot. Often the beating is self-inflicted. This was the easiest decision I've made in the last 2½ years!

Nora recognized that administration required her to deal with angry people and with conflict. She had discovered both something about the emotional dimensions of administrative leadership and, more important, something about herself, her capacity to lead amid interpersonal turbulence. She summarized her intrapersonal learning: "I can identify when my buttons are being pushed but I'm slow to identify the name of the button and choose an appropriate action." She continued, "When I consider my Myers-Briggs type, an ESFJ, I can see *why* I'm out of my realm when the issues are clouded by irrationality and deception." She had learned, as she put it, her "limits," the boundaries of her own capabilities *and* of her desire to push those limits for this new type of leadership job.

Her conclusion from this learning adventure is one that I find eminently mature and profound, not only for her but also for the leadership of her school. It is marked by deeper self-knowledge, richer knowledge about how leadership works, and above all an acknowledgment of the "comfort level" she needed to find in whatever leadership work she undertook.

> The overriding conclusion for me in the last few months is that I don't want to be sorting out all of the minutia and "magnutia" of school life, while I'm trying to figure out my place, my comfort level, in the realm of school leadership. I've arrived at this point with many regrets, but without a sense of failure. This position wasn't the right fit for me. . . .
>
> I have been a cheerleader and supporter for those who are willing to give back support as well as receive it; tried to depersonalize the tough decisions and make them with children in mind; respectfully met parents, students, and community members in difficult situations, setting boundaries with a sense of fairness; [and] tried to build and maintain a climate of respect for *all* the members of our school community, and I hope I've replanted a seed for the value of professional renewal among tired veterans.
>
> [I have] realized that being in a position of "authority and power" while maintaining my idea of collegial relationships (and friendships) is nearly impossible for *me*, and [the effort to do this] has been a source of constant intrapersonal and interpersonal struggle.

Nora returned to the classroom and her earlier role as respected teacher leader among her primary-grade colleagues. Her learning journey gave her greater confidence about her place as a leader. And this makes her experience emblematic of many others'. She found by exploring a new role a way to express her will to lead. For Nora and others, locating her place was a matter of seeing more clearly how her values and capabilities matched the leadership opportunities of her school.

FINDING THE "VALUES" FIT

Many leaders in our programs struggle with the presumed mantle of authority that comes with the term *leader*. In particular, they worry, as Nora did, about how their relationships with colleagues might change and about their own comfort levels with authority and, if they are considering administration, with power. These ponderings lead to intrapersonal questions that are, at their heart, about interpersonal and institutional ethics. The intrapersonal dialogue revolves around a basic question: If I need to lead like *this*, can I live with myself?

Earl, a new principal, echoed the tension Nora felt between "doing what I believe is right" and maintaining satisfactory relationships with faculty, concluding that he needed to learn how to exercise what he called "moral courage" even when it was likely to upset people:

> Moral courage is the most essential part of what I do . . . because
> it's so vital to do what's absolutely right. . . . Can I go home at night
> and know that I have done what's absolutely right? . . . My willing-
> ness [to act in this way] outweighed my ability to do this. . . . I
> always found myself oscillating between confidence and careful-
> ness in relationships with teachers.

In essence, Earl was learning how to walk one of the many narrow lines of the administrator's world. He was seeking a way to lead that met the high standards of his professional and personal values.

Professional ideals and values shape leaders' sense of what is right. Personal needs and values do, as well. Participants explored the tensions they felt between work and home, professional attainment and personal health. Intrapersonal learning, in this new sense, was an effort to establish a balance that was sustainable and healthy between leadership and self. Bill, a young first-year assistant principal, made these a centerpiece of his learning plan:

> Being able to make the statement "My family comes first" is easy.
> Living it is another issue. I feel as if I am constantly being pushed
> to go to one more meeting or be on one more committee; I feel
> that I am being judged on how valuable an administrator I am in
> those meetings. If I don't belong to these groups, I feel as if they
> are going to devalue me as a leader, as a professional, and as an
> individual. It appears that this situation ties itself to being secure in
> what you believe in and having the confidence to follow through
> with it even in the face of others who would criticize you for it. I

just hope sticking to my beliefs does not lead me down the wrong line. Namely, the unemployment line.

Fundamental questions such as these provoke intrapersonal learning because they induce self-examination, peering into why these leaders valued what they valued, why they had such strong feelings about how healthy relationships in schools should work. Borrowing from Osterman and Kottkamp (1993), Norris and colleagues (2002), and others, we call this "leadership platform" work: sorting out what you stand for and why. It is one of the core tasks of the intrapersonal learning domain.

For many, this involves studious examination of their beliefs about teaching, learning, school organization, and the role of authority. Often this leads to reaching down into their assumptions about how people should treat one another. Estelle, an emerging teacher leader, found in her ethnic heritage and family experience the roots of her own debates about using authority:

> I grew up in a very strict Franco-American Catholic environment. A large part of that upbringing viewed leaders as someone with a lot of power and authority. Take, for example, the parish priest. My grandmother . . . instilled in me that the priest was very powerful and all knowing. We were never to disagree with what the priest said. . . . This "fear" of people in authority extended to anyone (particularly men) who had an authoritative role. I was taught to never argue with those in authority.

Estelle's experience as a teacher and as a leader, however, convinced her that "leadership [that] works on some kind of fear" not only was unhealthy for schools but, further, was unhealthy for her. Her learning in our graduate program became a search "to uncover the basis for different leaders' leadership styles. . . . With this information, I can then hope to see a correlation between being a good leader and being authentic and true to oneself. As I go through this process of observation [of leaders] and reflection . . . I can begin to narrow down some leadership styles that will work for me."

The final stage in Estelle's learning journey, she stated,

> will be to find a leadership role to take on to try the different leadership styles I have learned through my observations and research. From there I can tweak the styles to fit my own authentic leadership style. Shakespeare was right on target when he wrote, "This above all: to thine own self be true, / And it must follow, as

the night the day, / Thou canst not then be false to any man" [*Hamlet* 1.3.75].

Herein lies the essence of the intrapersonal learning journey for many leaders: finding a sustainable fit between the leadership role they aspire to or currently occupy and their own values and beliefs as educators and as people. That is, finding a way to lead where they can authentically "walk their talk."

FINDING THE "CAPABILITY" FIT

Immersion in leadership work provokes another vital question: Am I capable of doing this work? The essence of intrapersonal learning in this respect engages the leader in assessing her or his temperament, skills, and knowledge and asking, "Do I have the right stuff for the leadership role I'm in or aspire to?" Nora's decision to step down from the teaching principalship was inspired largely by her realizations about herself and about the job that revealed to her that they were not suited to each other.

Reba, a teacher leader who became a successful high school principal, posed the "capability" question this way:

> I do have many concerns [about my journey toward a leadership role], perhaps more than I really had thought of. I also have fears that I need to work through. Some of those that immediately come to mind are
>
> - Will I be accepted as an official leader when the time comes?
> - Will I be able to delegate duties to others and give them the autonomy to do them?
> - Will I be able to diplomatically handle a task done in a method differently than I would have done it?
> - Ultimately, what does a leader do if people refuse to participate? What techniques can I employ to hopefully get team players?
> - Can I find, in myself, the strength to lead and not crumble when the tough times come?
> - Can I manage all the roles in life that are so important: wife, mother, professional, etc.?

We actively promote the pursuit of such questions. They push the leader's self-understanding in a very direct way. They generate practical inquiry that demands honest answers, answers that are tied to one's capacity to lead. The intrapersonal learning agendas that emerge give rise to an important expectation in our programs: that successful leaders know where their talents do and do not lie.

The exploration of "fit" always involves "me" and "the job." Intrapersonally, this means learning about "who I am" and learning what personal qualities and capabilities leadership demands of a person. One teacher leader, Ruth, was weighing both of these when she reflected:

> I am becoming somewhat comfortable with the idea that, when in a leadership role, uncertainty, change, and the whirlwind atmosphere tend to be the norm rather than the abnormal. I prefer the concrete sequential orderliness of things, but I am working to live in the more flexible, changing world, outside the safety of the four walls of the classroom. . . .
>
> I used to think that I was a natural leader. Since I have become a member of the MSLN group, I realize that other people who have placed me in a leadership role might think the SJ manager traits [from the Myers-Briggs Type Inventory] that I naturally possess allowing me to complete tasks, follow rules, organize, and follow through allow the group to function well under my leadership.
>
> MSLN group discussions, the MBTI, Colleague-Critic Team meetings, conversations with [my MSLN coach], and soul searching reflective practice have allowed me to ask some deep questions [about how my "get-it-done" skill set can undercut the] interpersonal skills I need to create effective relationships and collaboration." . . . [I am now focused on learning how I] must work to balance all areas to form effective relationships.

We make available a number of self-assessment options for leaders to use, as Ruth did, to gauge their capabilities. (See I-C-I assessment criteria in the Appendix.) These generate "working hypotheses" about a leader's qualities and capabilities. When used in combination with reflection-on-action and reflective protocols, these hypotheses can be tested "in the real world" and the results can give leaders good insight into themselves.

Feedback is also a powerful stimulus to intrapersonal reflection and learning. Leaders, new and old, work in worlds with astoundingly little direct feedback. Colleagues who see, hear, and feel leaders' performance are a potent source of feedback. As Ruth notes, these descriptions of how a leader's performance looked "to someone I'm trying to lead" generated deep questions for participants. Here, the interpersonal "data" from colleagues spawned intrapersonal exploration, usually aimed at grasping more fully how the leader could adapt her or his interactions with colleagues. That is, growing self-awareness was usually linked to greater skills at self-management in action.

Irving, an assistant principal, had a tendency, particularly when he felt defensive, to say things that led to hard feelings, misunderstandings, and relational uncertainty among his staff. He found this in-house coaching invaluable to his intrapersonal learning:

> I felt that thinking out loud was my "style." Myers-Briggs confirmed observations of me by critical friends and my own introspection. Not thinking enough about the results of what I say has gotten me into more hot water than all the defensive nonlistening and other behaviors put together. Clearly, this needs to be a major point of emphasis [for my learning] and has not been.
>
> I continue to debrief with Emma after meetings. She frequently scripts them. We meet at least once a week now to review each other's progress. I am logging the first 5 seconds of most defensive conversations whether by type of encounter or by logging the phrase that got me. I am trying to take time to decompress after being yelled at.

Another way to learn about personal assets and challenges is to videotape or audiotape yourself "leading live," for example, facilitating a meeting, leading a staff activity, consulting over a difficult problem. Nancy, an aspiring principal, videotaped herself teaching a lesson in her elementary classroom and leading a staff work session on the writing process. Earlier feedback had made her wonder if her rate and patterns of talk were hindering her effectiveness. Comparing herself in the two settings, she decided:

> The comfort levels for me and the participants were drastically different in the two situations. During the student lesson, my comfort level, and hopefully the students', was very high. During the staff presentation the setup was uncomfortable from the start. It was designed as a sit-and-get meeting. The topic was a touchy one. It was school board directed: We had to do it. . . .
>
> I was shocked at the lack of language skill I demonstrated when I looked at the staff presentation on paper. The words in isolation are not coherent. Yuck. It also emphasizes to me how important the other elements of the presentation are. The paralanguage and body language saved the presentation from being completely incoherent.

Unbelievable. This will definitely impact how I prepare for [future presentations and meetings].

Nancy created a rating scale to monitor her performance in future facilitation roles focusing on how she used words and especially the rate at which she talked. She concluded: "All in all, I need to be more aware of my audience and plan my use of language better."

Educators in our programs used opportunities like these to see themselves authentically. As challenging as it was to seek feedback for teacher leaders and administrators alike, the benefits were often tangible. Feedback shed the light of reality on their ambitions; as Howie, a veteran high school principal, put it, "My behavior *is* affected by how I feel." They saw more clearly how their skills in certain situations worked well but how, in other circumstances, they might not. And they saw how knowing their assets and liabilities as people and as educators was essential to finding a leadership role that they could fulfill *and* that was fulfilling for them.

CAN I MANAGE THE PERSONAL CHALLENGES OF LEADERSHIP?

Ultimately, the leadership learning journey circles back to the place it began: Do I want to do this kind of work? It's a question that every leader needs to revisit periodically, as effective leadership is far more likely from committed, eager leaders than it is from ambivalent or tired leaders. Giving leaders a chance to revisit the question in light of their own experience, we find, can be extraordinarily powerful. From it comes a clarified and renewed sense of what is possible for each person to accomplish as a leader—*what is sustainable and productive for both the leader and the school.* Failure to achieve "fit" in this sense can readily cause a leader to feel "wounded," a condition that Ackerman and Maslin-Ostrowski (2002) note is healthy for neither the leader nor the school.

We encourage our learning colleagues to explore as many different leadership templates and descriptors of leader qualities as they can (for example, Starratt's conception of ethical leadership, 2004, or the Interstate School Leader Licensure Consortium standards, 1996). They examine them, debate them, apply them to colleagues at work, and try them on for size. They usually find these cognitive frameworks idealized, overwhelming, and difficult to link to their own performance. Often, though, they become useful when one small skill or strategy in them suddenly comes alive in their own practice. As Ted said, "I need to personalize this." Seeing how their own efforts to match the ideal do or don't generate productive responses from their colleagues shows them the way *they* can lead.

These intrapersonal lessons are lessons in self-awareness and self-management. They are lessons born of growing self-awareness and growing understanding of the process of mobilization. In part, leaders' maturation involves coming to terms with their limitations. Confirmation, however, comes when the cues from their colleagues and surroundings begin to show them their own fit with a role that is productive for them and for those around them.

Tim was a high school assistant principal who, a year into our program, came to the realization that his job could be deeply "demoralizing" for him. Teachers and parents second-guessed his decisions, often leaving him wondering whether it's ever possible to be successful as a principal in the eyes of all constituencies: "Their second-guessing of me can have a rippling effect on my ability to do my job and adds to my anxiety issues. How do I deal with all of this? . . . My job is probably one of the toughest jobs in education and I'm not sure if I have the 'right stuff' to continue in this role."

In his journey through the graduate program and beyond, Tim worked hard to find an answer to this "do I fit" conundrum. He thought a lot about his values and knowledge base in an effort to gain "more confidence in my decisions." And he began to be more planful in his personal life to "take better care of my physical health." Tim learned, in this process, to make sure that he was "involved with positive activities" at school, counteracting the deleterious effects of "no-win" tasks that tended to drag him down.

Eventually, he transferred to a position as elementary principal where, away from the politics of high school and the intense emotions of adolescents, he thrived among the many "positive activities" he helped to create and celebrate. He was able, through his deeper awareness of his values, his personality, and his skills, to "manage himself" into a leadership role where he could be more productive and happier.

Self-awareness and self-management, the two great outcomes of intrapersonal learning, often generate a deeper sense of self-efficacy for leaders. Theresa came to MSLN uncertain whether she wanted to continue in the role of teacher leader that she had grown into over years of extraordinary work in her elementary school. She was exhausted, "losing focus . . . losing my balance." She was wondering if the sort of servant leadership she'd developed was productive for the school *and* sustainable for her. Here is how she described the emergence of her own template for self-management:

I started writing about my hectic life [in journals]. Through several colleague-critic team meetings and with help from [my MSLN coach] I wrote a Leadership Development Plan [LDP]. By working out some filtering questions, I [now] can more clearly assert my voice and my needs as well as maintain a leadership role at [my school]. At present my filtering questions are these:

1. Does this activity/role/course/committee fit in with my other commitments? (Remember them all, Theresa!) In regard to time, how many meetings—monthly, weekly, long term, short term?
2. Does it provide me with new learning or insight?
3. Does it excite me?
4. Does it fit in with my vision for school improvement or my LDP?
5. If I add it to my commitments, what will I let go?

Theresa's leadership development plan was, for her, a self-management plan to protect her from being consumed by her professional commitments and drive. It is still in use today, guiding her ongoing but now more sustainable work as teacher leader.

Unlike Theresa, Kathleen, a guidance counselor, entered our graduate program with a tendency to feel she was already a leader who had many of the answers.

I came into the cohort cocky, on the crest of the wave [thinking I could do this leadership stuff]. But part way in, *underneath* the wave, a lot of the assumptions I'd made were needing questions asked. For example, that I knew a lot about education and how it should be done. . . . I was thinking through *things* [programs, goals, change strategies] instead of taking people where they are. . . . But I wasn't seeing leadership this way when I started.

Her intrapersonal journey took her, as she put it, from "unconscious incompetence to conscious incompetence," a transition she saw as vital to her leadership effectiveness because it opened the way, ultimately, to "conscious competence":

I came to see my learning as a Slinky, because it works in a spiral. It begins with unconscious incompetence becoming conscious incompetence through a process of reflection, examining assumptions, and asking hard questions. Then it moves to learning *about* things, the cognitive learning, [because] I'm an external processor. And then I need to do a lot of experimenting with things—the interpersonal side.

Moving from "unconscious" to "conscious" describes aptly what intrapersonal learning is all about: stimulating the greater self-awareness that is essential to self-management; moving from self-ascribed effectiveness to authenticated efficacy. As educators understand more fully what their own leadership capabilities and goals are—more fully in the sense that they have seen in their own experience "what works for me"—they sense their place and identity in the leadership mix of their schools. In Kathleen's terminology, they have emerged into greater "conscious competence and conscious incompetence."

For the many seasoned educators who come to our leadership programs, this intrapersonal learning journey is ripe for the running. They have scads of experience and many models, some not so good and some not so bad, of colleagues who have attempted to lead. Our program, structured as it is to examine the cognitive, interpersonal, and intrapersonal dimensions, gives them permission to seek their own understandings of what works and to use them to develop their own means of self-management as leaders.

Connie, a widely respected informal teacher leader in her high school, summarized this transformation nicely:

> [When we started the Maine Academy for School Leaders (MASL)] . . . on one level I had no idea what I expected [to get from the experience]; I wasn't even sure if I belonged in this group. On another more instinctive level, though, I knew why I was there: I needed to become more confident in myself as a leader. It is interesting for me to look back at the notes from that meeting; next to my comment is the word *informal* in parentheses.
>
> At this point [at the end of the program] I see that I was in a transitional stage. I viewed myself as a teacher who had influence over other people, a kind of de facto leader, but I hadn't yet acknowledged or come to a full realization of my formal role as a leader in our school. [MASL has been for me] my transitional journey which is, to a large degree, the journey of how I have come to accept myself as a legitimate, formal school leader. Underpinning this self-acceptance is the confidence I have developed in myself as a leader.

THE ESSENCE OF INTRAPERSONAL LEARNING

Our colleagues have taught us much about the process of deepening intra-personal knowledge. It is not always an easy journey. Many of our colleagues came to our leadership program unaware of its importance or, at least, not expecting that a graduate program would entertain the vital personal questions and lessons that the choice to lead raises. Pursuing them, as Heifetz and Linsky (2004) report, takes persistence, honesty, and courage.

Some of our colleagues struggled to make the sorts of intrapersonal gains that the examples in this chapter have illustrated. For some, the reluctance to look inward ran very deep. Or the climate and relationships within the program cohort were insufficiently safe. Or our emphasis on the intrapersonal and interpersonal were so foreign to them intellectually and philosophically that they required too much effort for too little benefit. Some, I think, lacked the disposition to look inward and appraise themselves in light of leadership requirements.

But for most, the unlocking effects of intrapersonal learning were profound. By coming to understand that their motives, and capacities, to lead were essential determinants of their ability to perform as leaders, they gained a level of control, confidence, and self-efficacy as leaders. As is true with learning in the interpersonal and the cognitive domains, *intrapersonal growth happens most when integrated with learning in the other two domains*. That is, growth came from realizing that they alone could not "will" best practice upon their colleagues and their school. Instead, leadership would emerge from their own artful self-conduct and their ability to remain sensitive to their own interpersonal effects.

Leadership, if it was to emerge from their efforts at all, would flower from the knowledge, beliefs, and efforts of the group, not singly from them. In this respect, intrapersonal learning stems from a multistage process:

1. Clarifying the beliefs and values I hold about effective learning, effective teaching, effective school organization, and effective working relationships and assuring myself that these are supported by a valid knowledge base (cognitive)
2. Understanding how I act with and react to others and how my skills shape my working relationships and thus my capacity to mobilize others to action (interpersonal)
3. Determining where my "areas of challenge" lie with reference to both my cognitive and interpersonal knowledge base
4. Drawing on my assessments of assets and liabilities to locate a fitting leadership role that I know makes a positive difference for students and staff and is personally sustainable for me.

The intrapersonal domain held powerful lessons for many because it legitimized the feelings, doubts, and affirming moments of aspiring leaders. When explored within a collegial circle where support and advice were abundant, participants had a means to think through why they sought to lead and to ascertain if their will to lead was sufficient to the task of leading well. Finally, intrapersonal exploration gave them the confidence of knowing where their strengths lay and, just as important, where they did not.

Vi, a middle school teacher leader, summarized it for many:

What lies within me is a keen understanding of who I am as a leader and a person. I have an articulated platform [of beliefs about education and leadership]; clearly embraced values and goals; and a keen appreciation for the talents, strengths, skills, and limitations I possess. I make no apologies for my gentle spirit; because of it, not in spite of it, I have defined myself as a leader.

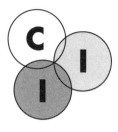

CHAPTER 7

Coming to Know I Can Lead

> There was no right or wrong way to lead a ship and a squadron—every captain had his own approach, depending on his talents and temperament. . . . But if the officers' and crews' expectations should go unfulfilled in any significant or even insignificant way, the complex interpersonal chemistry of a crowded ship could be quickly and irrevocably altered, transforming a vessel that had once operated like a well-oiled machine into a pressure cooker about to explode.
>
> —Nat Philbrick, *Sea of Glory*

HOW DOES A LEADER KNOW she or he is leading? For Captain Charles Wilkes, who in 1848, at age 37, found himself the commander of a U.S. naval expedition of six ships, the question resounds, just as it does for leaders of schools. There is no right or wrong way, but there are better and worse ways. And woe betide any leader who, in the process of learning to lead, loses her or his "officers and crew."

Nat Philbrick, the author of *Sea of Glory*, about Wilkes's early career, explains Wilkes's initial strategy as leader:

> In the beginning, Wilkes seems to have employed the only command style with which he had any recent experience—the genial approach. . . . He . . . [dined] with his officers [and] . . . frequently left his cabin to socialize in the Vincennes's wardroom. As if to distract himself from the immensity of the

challenges ahead, he directed his attention to the more easily managed details of shipboard life. (Philbrick, 2003, p. 68)

School leaders, too, enter the world of leadership surrounded by numerous opinions of "the right or wrong way" to lead. As Charles Wilkes
found, it is natural to begin leadership by taking the "genial approach."
For many, early success and personal satisfaction lie in taking on "the more
easily managed details" of school life. But how does a school leader come
to know that her or his attempts at leading are *really* productive for the
school?

In this chapter I explore the essential question, How do I know I'm
leading? It is the core question for learning leaders—and for every leadership development program. It's impossible to judge whether learning activities have taken hold without asking, What is the evidence that this
learning has made me a better leader?

While many leadership programs use leadership inventories, skills
assessment, and cognitive recall to assess leaders' learning gains, we find
there is no substitute for looking directly at effects on staff and students to
see evidence of leadership success. Unless he had taken to the seas, Charles
Wilkes would never have stumbled upon the shortcomings of the "genial
approach" or have learned that attending only to "the more easily managed details of shipboard life" was certain to lead his fleet astray. Three
primary methods of determining learning and leadership impact were
helpful in our programs: examining evidence based on self-observations,
on educational outcomes, and on colleagues' observations and feedback.

DO MY ACTIONS CREATE SOMETHING I'D CALL LEADERSHIP?

Leaders pondering their effectiveness naturally compare themselves to
the ideal. They test their own performance against conceptions of leaders from experience, their reading, and from colleagues. When there's a
fit, learners feel reinforced. When there isn't, uncertainty grows: "Is it
me? Am I really 'leadership stuff'? Or is my blueprint of what leaders do
wrong?"

This implicit comparison winds its way through many of the learning stories in this book, pointing the learner constantly back to her or his
own work at school in search of evidence. Dinah, a teacher leader, had
grown disheartened by the negativity and defeatism among some of her
colleagues at school. Early on, she saw this as "the principal's problem"
since he "was the only one who could address it." As she examined it and
thought more about her own role, with the help of a book by Kegan and

Lahey (2001), Dinah began to see in her own behaviors some evidence of leadership potential:

> I want to have healthy relationships [among the adults in our school]. . . . I know that one tool for achieving healthy relationships is using straight talk . . . good communication . . . and that one way to undercut healthy relationships is complaining, griping, and gossiping. . . . Taking the advice of Kegan and Lahey and my [colleague-critic team], I am going to watch myself in this area.
>
> I've already been in three situations where I would have reverted to gossiping and whining, but I consciously didn't. I tried to think about what I would have said in the past and how that would have contributed to the conversation. I realized that I would only feed the flames. . . .
>
> [Instead], I actively listened to the conversation and watched the players. I realized that they are really unhappy people! Or, at least, they sounded unhappy. On the other hand, their complaints showed what they valued. . . . This helped me realize that to get a group of people to stop this kind of talk, they need to be helped to voice their complaints in a useful, productive way. . . . This has become the focus of my next [Leadership Development Plan].

In subsequent months, Dinah's journal entries charted her colleagues' reactions when she stopped contributing to the "gossiping and whining" and began to assert the position that they all should turn complaint into problem solving. It was a turning point for her self-concept as a leader as well as for her position among her colleagues. She had begun not only to act like the leader she aspired to be but also to have her colleagues acknowledge this change.

Nan, a teacher leader, made a similar discovery. Her Leadership Development Plan focused on monitoring responses to her leadership in meetings and learning to use this immediate evidence to modulate her own behaviors:

> I discovered that I could decrease [my] feelings of intimidation if I kept scanning the room making eye contact with everybody. I felt more confident doing that because I perceived it made me look more confident. It also kept me from focusing on the people who seemed distant or disinterested. . . . When I asked for feedback [from committee members], they described me as clear and confident without shutting people off.

Understanding how one's own leadership efforts are playing out in real situations requires intrapersonal frankness and the ability to observe oneself in action—what Ronald Heifetz (1994) aptly terms "getting on the balcony." Many participants in our programs feel overwhelmed at first. They enter with many questions about how leadership works. The varied issues, people, and emotions of their own schools are confusing, even chaotic. They haven't developed a sufficient vocabulary yet for describing the to-and-fro of interaction and deliberation in their own leadership situations. Cognitive frameworks such as Kegan and Lahey's (2001), Bolman and Deal's (2005), and the I-C-I model itself give them lenses for sorting out these dynamics "from the balcony."

For the more successful, the growing capacity to accurately understand their school contexts helps them to see their own leadership possibilities. Theo, an aspiring principal, wrote in his summative narrative:

At the very beginning of my [leadership activities in my school], I discovered my tendency to be an isolated and narrow-minded decision maker. . . . It is not that I am a bully and have nothing to contribute, it is simply that I tend to become a bit too passionate in my commitment and see only my way as the right way. . . . I was feeling that it was my responsibility alone to have all the answers *and* that I had them!

Theo drew on evidence he was seeing about his own "walk" to see how he was successfully engaging some colleagues on his middle-level team, but not others. From this assessment, he created a learning plan to "remedy" his weakness:

[I now see that] I'm not walking my talk about shared decision-making. My belief is . . . that leaders must "maximize their human resources by bringing out the experience and knowledge of everyone in the group." But in my middle-level team, I tend to get very territorial with projects/programs that I develop. From this reflection, I focused on adopting some roles [in team meetings] designed to combat this negative behavior such as becoming a better listener and as a solicitor of feedback.

Literature and inventories that frame specific images and skills of leader behavior often helped our colleagues assess their own efforts. The application of this cognitive learning to specific incidents generated bits and pieces of evidence that informed future learning and action steps. Ruth's reflection showed her that she tended to "tune certain people out, especially if they were not being clear or precise" or wanted to "talk and talk and talk about the issue." It showed her, too, that these same people tended not to respond to her leadership. From this, she generated a new ideal for herself: "I feel [that leaders] must be able to listen, really listen, to what group members have to say. I need to improve myself in this area so that others will see me as a caring, respectful person that values their input."

Ruth consulted with her facilitator and colleagues and read a number of articles. One listed guidelines for empathetic listening. She used these behaviors as a model to alter her own behavior in a subsequent meeting at school:

> I am sitting, actually leaning toward the person speaking, and making eye contact with the speaker, and smiling in a friendly manner to make sure the speaker feels more confident and secure. I have come a long way. . . . The values "I am responsible for my actions" and "I don't have the power to change others, only myself" guide me when I communicate with others.

Our programs require regular reflective journal writing and other methods of debriefing experience such as critical incident protocols (Brookfield, 1995) or "peeling the onion" protocols (Korthagen & Vasalos, 2005). Reflective writing and analyses kept the essential question, Am I actually leading? in front of our learners. While their own assessments provided a flow of valuable ideas and self-observations, they suffered the inevitable shortcomings of all self-assessments. Leaders are usually not the best independent judges of their own effects on others (Boyatzis et al., 1995). In the end, leaders need evidence from beyond themselves. They need to know if their efforts at leadership are contributing to "results" that matter to children, parents, teachers, and their districts.

AM I MAKING A DIFFERENCE FOR CHILDREN?

Many would argue that the best test of leadership is whether it produces healthy development and rich learning for students. I agree. But taking the measure of your leadership by documenting its impacts on students and their learning is far more difficult to do than it is to declare them. So many "variables," as they say, "intervene" between the leader and "student outcomes" that you can rarely say definitively, My leadership made that happen.

We believe, however, that it is essential that leaders' seek evidence of their impacts—good and bad—on the school's learners. We have found that such evidence is more retrievable and credible when the leader's efforts are trained on specific student outcomes. We require our learning leaders to frame their learning within a plan to lead—an initiative or goal for student growth where the participant is working with an identifiable group of people within a general time frame. Within this arena, they write "action goals" as leaders: what they are trying to accomplish for students and how they are likely to know whether they're making progress toward these goals. Here are two examples:

> Jeanne, a newly appointed science department chair, sought to put in place a mechanism for the science teachers to analyze the results of state achievement tests and to use them to focus their teaching on areas needing improvement.

> Evan, also a newly appointed department chair, chose to focus on the newly hired English teacher and ways to help her develop effective teaching practices aimed at specific student learning outcomes.

A couple of things are important about these plans to lead. They provide the leader with a more focused picture of what she or he is trying to accomplish than that leader had before writing it down. They help the leader articulate how and why the changes in practice she or he is proposing to colleagues should create conditions for better student learning. In this fashion, an implementation plan can be co-owned and co-created by colleagues and constituents, enhancing prospects for successful mobilization.

What's important for the leader's learning, though, is that the plan to lead has fairly clear statements of learning outcomes for children. They can focus on any aspect of the school's learning mission that the leader and her or his colleagues value: increasing math computation skills, growing "mediation skills" among classroom leaders, developing higher-order thinking in writing, improving the success rate on AP exams.

These goal statements give the leader a set of criteria for assessing effectiveness at leading. Jeanne's written action plan, for example, gave her a baseline for assessing her impacts. Four months into her leadership development work, she wrote:

> Another piece of evidence [of my learning] came from the science team. Using a data protocol [that I introduced them to], they analyzed their MEA [state achievement test] results. This had a twofold effect. First, it allowed the science team to assess the use of a protocol in analyzing data. Second, it allowed the science team to

really look at the MEA scores with improvement in mind. . . . [For a next step,] I plan to administer an assessment continuum to the science team and myself that will help us look at where we are using these results with our students.

Evan had worked closely with Stella, a new teacher, whose success with students was at risk. His Leadership Development Plan focused on his own effectiveness in this all-important supervisory role:

Now that I look back on this semester, my work with Stella falls into four phases: observing, planning, acting, and reflecting. Before I did anything, I observed the situation and attempted to give it shape and context by listening to what others—students, teachers, guidance counselors, and parents—had to say about the difficulties Stella and her students were having. I planned and acted when I realized that something had to be done—when I realized that the situation was not self-rectifying. I reflected with others—the principal, Giselle, and Stella—to come up with workable solutions. . . . And the result has been that she has prepared lessons plans that include systems of positive reinforcement for the students who were finding her too demanding and unresponsive to them when they felt overwhelmed.

These entries mark two aspects of the leadership-assessment process that pester learning leaders. One is the difficulty that leaders have in tracking the impacts on students through their work with staff members. The other is that seeing impacts on students takes time and is often difficult to measure. Jeanne succeeded at getting the science team to analyze assessment test scores, but that does not yet mean that those teachers will use those data to improve the learning of students who are experiencing difficulty. By the same token, Evan's initial success helping Stella adjust her practice to accommodate some students who were struggling doesn't yet mean that those students will learn better.

Although frustrated by the complexities of tracking their own impacts as leaders through to students, Jeanne, Evan, and most of our participants came to understand how essential it was to hold this high standard for themselves. The programs try to support these efforts by requiring regular reflective journaling, using "critical incident" protocols to trace immediate impacts of their activities, and holding "taking stock" sessions every 4 months where leaders bring "evidence of impacts" and help one another assess it.

While leaders in our programs can understandably never claim all the credit for improving student learning, they present in their periodic portfolios summaries of their activities, descriptions of actions emerging from these activities taken by colleagues and others, and "student data" that are associated with these new actions. This three-stage framework usually yields much more evidence of leader activities and colleague actions than it does of student impacts, but this assessment process sets the compass for ongoing monitoring of leader effects. It also thrusts our learning leaders into assessment activities with their colleagues that make the entire instructional enterprise more data-driven.

It bears repeating that the "real leadership arenas" are absolutely essential to the development of "real" learning—learning that helps our colleagues authentically understand their effects as leaders. In recent years, evidence of impacts from our colleagues' learning-and-action efforts has come in three major varieties:

1. Improvement of specific practices that show benefits to students through documented changes in practice and in student learning, attitudes, and behavior. For example:

    • A teacher leader and a principal worked together to involve their entire middle school in a literacy program, changing the grouping and instructional practices and measuring changes in student performance.
    • A teacher leader led her grade-level team in revamping math curriculum, instruction, and assessment, including learning to look together at assessment results and to use them for reteaching.
    • Three teacher leaders in the same school lead a staff development effort to engage faculty and parents in addressing issues of student harassment, including period scanning and surveys to monitor it.
    • An assistant principal engaged faculty in training for and planning student-led conferences across the high school, carrying them out, and assessing their impact for parents and for students.

2. Advocacy for student-focused change through voicing significant needs and mobilizing others to take steps toward meeting them. For example:

    • The leader of a secondary alternative education program successfully negotiated the approval and construction of a facility for the 50-plus students her program is keeping in school.

- An elementary school curriculum specialist convinced administrators to develop more effective ways of giving classroom teachers access to the expertise and support of specialists.
- A teacher leader reversed the "negative direction" of a districtwide math initiative through brokering a new understanding among five schools and the assistant superintendent.
- A special educator in one school and an educational technician in another successfully drew attention to wasteful practices in the roles, duties, and supervision of ed techs.

3. Building leadership capacity by mobilizing colleagues to more powerful professional learning, instructional improvement, and student assessment for their schools. For example:

- An elementary school principal used her own experience with professional portfolios to lead her school and district to a new teacher appraisal system.
- Three teacher leaders from rural school led a 2-year strategic planning effort for staff and community that generated a more focused professional learning agenda for staff and better relations with community.
- A high school principal and teacher leader facilitated team-building and visioning in their faculty, resulting in consensus for change and a grant application to support it.
- Several leaders from the same district helped their administrative team develop stronger skills and norms for professional problem solving and planning; this effort facilitated the creation of a powerful local assessment and standard-setting process for all schools.

DO THOSE I SEEK TO LEAD SEE ME AS A LEADER?

The third approach to assessing leader effectiveness springs from a simple proposition: If those whom you seek to lead tell you that you are leading them, then you probably are! Here, evidence of leadership is evidence that the leader's efforts are taking hold with those people who are essential to the school's success with children: the faculty and staff. After all, a school can hardly shine if a leader's place in "the complex interpersonal chemistry of [the school is] quickly and irrevocably altered, transforming [the] vessel that had once operated like a well-oiled machine into a pressure cooker about to explode" (Philbrick, 2003, p. 68).

Leaders engaged in this form of assessment look to their colleagues for feedback. They open themselves to the impressions, opinions, and judgments of those colleagues regarding the outcomes and the processes of their leadership. Often, as we saw in Chapter 5, this is the most valid and useful way to understand one's interpersonal qualities as they are experienced by others.

For many, this is very difficult work. Few participants have worked with leaders who have openly sought feedback about their leadership. Our program includes skill development exercises and resources for seeking, hearing, and using feedback. They all require practice with familiar, trusted colleagues before they are used in "real life." Specific protocols for structuring a feedback interview are helpful to many (Glaude, 2005; McDonald, 1996). Participants also find useful commercially available "360-degree feedback" devices such as the Leadership Profile Inventory (Kouzes & Posner, 2007) and homemade written surveys seeking feedback on specific aspects of leadership performance of interest to the leader.

Participants usually start by soliciting colleagues' observations of their performance, focused on the behaviors identified in the goals of their Leadership Development Plans. As they grow comfortable hearing feedback and find colleagues at work and in the program who are comfortable giving feedback, their assessments become more targeted, frequent, and natural. More generalized and structured assessments are safer for most and thus are initially more popular. Micky, a new principal, wrote about the feedback she received using the Leadership Profile Inventory:

> I have come to value the objective perspectives I gain through trusted colleagues who enrich the way I see things. . . . Alone I would not come to the same conclusion. . . . Self-reflection is good but limited without the honest perspectives of others who are trusted. . . .
>
> The results of the Leadership Profile Inventory cemented this shift. I had to face the fact that my perspective alone was incomplete. . . . There was no denying it: Input from others gave me a more balanced assessment of who I was at work and how I was experienced by others in the context of the work I did. I began to address this as I worked to limit the wasted energy I expended on [my] misperceptions [of myself]. I pushed myself to seek and listen to outside feedback.

Soliciting and using feedback from participants in specific leadership episodes allowed participants to ask directly how aspects of the episode played out for them. The more concrete a person's leadership plan and Leadership Development Plan are, the more focused and helpful the feedback can be. As one teacher leader put it, "This was an opportunity to experiment with the new leader ideas and behaviors that our LDPs [Leadership Development Plans] set up. . . . The portfolio is like our first lab report, with the LDP as the hypothesis that we've been trying to test. Feedback from others is what helps us know how well that hypothesis has worked."

Some used a brief feedback form or debriefing format with participants at the end of meetings or asked a colleague to serve as an observer during a meeting and sit with them afterward to debrief. Nan, a teacher leader who was seeking to be more assertive as a facilitator, wrote:

> People told me that they had seen me use straight talk in meetings. . . . [They] noticed my use of straight talk. Some of the comments they specifically noted were "I am calling this meeting to order"; "Tell me what you want"; "Talk to us about that."

Freda, a special education codirector, was trying to be more consultative with her staff and less "the boss." Following a conference with a teacher who had a reputation for being difficult, she found in the teacher's feedback confirmation of her own progress:

> Although the meeting was long, I felt she was relieved about the meeting. She expressed that for the first time in her 15-year placement in the district, she feels she is being supported. She stated that [the way I worked with her didn't make her] feel reprimanded or told to take care of the problem herself but rather she felt supported and guided to be a better teacher. . . . I could not have been happier. I think by using the active listening skills I have learned in this class, I was able to overcome the "boss" stigma and gain a "leader" profile.

Freda's example illustrates how feedback from colleagues can inquire directly into how staff are experiencing the leader's interactions with them and into how those interactions are assisting or hindering the staff member's work with children. Here is the essential linkage between leader, staff member, and student learning.

As leaders become more open to feedback and more skilled at soliciting it, they learn to "see myself through their eyes," as one principal put it. They also learn to evaluate their own relationships and interaction patterns with individuals and groups. We attempt to nurture this skill by having colleagues and staff observe one another in simulated situations and occasionally in "real leadership" in their schools. In MSLN and Maine Academy for School Leaders, full-time staff facilitators regularly met participants in their schools to observe and confer, developing the type of ongoing reflective dialogues about practice that we will see illustrated by Vlade and Patience in Chapter 8. We as staff sought to model this vital process by seeking feedback on our leadership from participants and pursuing our own Leadership Development Plans as well.

MAKING SENSE OF THE EVIDENCE: THE POWERS OF REFLECTION

These three sources of evidence—self-observation, impacts on students and programs, and impacts on staff colleagues—offer up a rich stew to the learning leader. Inevitably, it's incomplete and dynamic, bubbling with subjectivity and tentativeness. We often hear such comments as, "This is all so ambiguous. Aren't there any rules to follow?" Our response is that, because each of us is different and works amid a different set of people and relationships, we each need to adapt how we learn to the needs of the school and to our own uniqueness as individuals. The central rule is, *Learn from your school how you can help to lead it.*

Monitoring success as a leader comes down to one's powers of reflection, to leaders' capacity to address two questions:

- How did my efforts in this case contribute to mobilizing others?
- What did this teach me about where I need to focus my next effort?

We refer to this retrospective analysis as reflection-on-action. Our goal, however, is not only to nurture reflection-on-action skills, but also to support leaders to reflect "in action"—to build their capacities to make sense *while the action is occurring* so that they can adapt their own leadership efforts to be more immediately productive. These constitute what I call performance learning: learning through our own performance. Fortunately, a rich literature is growing around this vital dimension of professional learning (Drago-Severson, 2004; Hopkins, 1994; Osterman, 1998; Schön, 1983; Sternberg & Horvath, 1999).

Figure 7.1 shows one way to think about the process of making sense of leadership evidence. It encompasses the three methods of collecting evidence described in this chapter and anchors these in the central theater of leadership, the "action" of the leader's actual performance.

FIGURE 7.1. Evidence and Questions for Reflective Learning

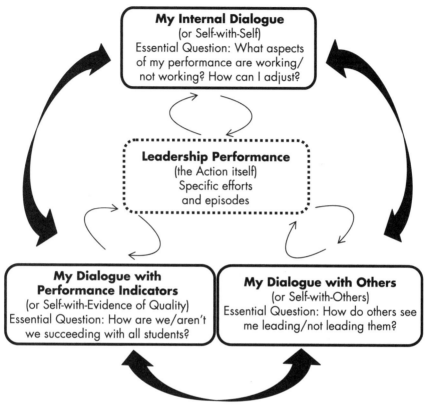

Effective leaders listen to their schools, to their colleagues and constituents, and to themselves. As they grow more sophisticated at asking each of the essential questions in Figure 7.1, they are better able to judge how their intentions (self) are shaped by their relationships with colleagues (others) on their way to making a difference in the school's effectiveness with students (school). Through this process we promote a model of effective leadership that binds the leader's understanding of her- or himself (self-self) to evidence of the school's performance (self-school) and of the roles that her or his relationships with significant others (self-other) plays in her or his success.

Most of the leader writing in this book is the product of this kind of reflection. It illustrates how the I-C-I domains offer a language for analyzing evidence from the three sources and for fashioning goals for learning from it. The cognitive lens applies largely but not exclusively to *dialogue with Dialogue Performance Indicators: How is my own cognitive knowledge base affecting my and colleagues' success at improving children's learning?* How are our efforts informed or not by relevant information on learning, teaching, and organizational matters? How are my own contributions to this effort enhanced or constrained by my own knowledge base? What could I learn before the next meeting that would strengthen my contribution? As one teacher leader said, "The cohort [program] kept helping us see how what we're reading is wrapping around what we're living."

Dialogue with Others generates interpersonal evidence *informing leaders' understanding of their interpersonal capacity to monitor, adjust to, and shape relationships.* What does so-and-so's response tell me about his commitment to this project and his relationships within the team and to me? What does the feedback I heard at the end tell me about the readiness of these people to engage in this work with me? How did my own actions provoke responses in others and were these productive or not? What can I learn and do before the next meeting that would strengthen my contribution?

Finally, leaders' *Internal Dialogues* call out their *capacity to "read" how they are feeling, how they are making sense of events and people, and how these are influencing their words and behaviors as they are performing.* Was I fully aware of my own reactions and able to manage them for the benefit of the group's effort and goal? Were there moments when I could have participated differently than I did? Am I feeling committed to this work and to my colleagues? What can I learn and do before the next meeting that would strengthen my contribution?

The consummate skill for leaders is the ability to immediately adjust to cognitive, interpersonal, and intrapersonal cues in the leadership situation. This capacity for reflection-in-action permits the leader to run a videotape in the back of her mind asking, What do I see, hear, feel, taste, and smell in this room that tells me I'm actually leading? This is the ability to "get on the balcony" and to observe "the dance" on the floor below even as you, the leader, participate in that dance (Heifetz, 1994). It involves learning to make sense of what you observe in the school's performance, in your colleagues, and in yourself and to use that to reinforce or alter your own patterns of leadership behavior accordingly.

Others have explored the richness of such leader reflection as an essential component for assessing effectiveness and cultivating new skills and capacities (Argyris, 1993; Goleman et al., 2002; Lave & Wenger, 1991; Sternberg & Horvath, 1999). David Kolb's (1984) Experiential Learning Theory model helps identify how concrete experience, abstract conceptualization, reflective observation, and active experimentation interact in professional learning. Kolb, Boyatzis, and Mainemelis (2000) extend this work. These scholars reinforce our own observation that the learner's involvement in "real leadership" is absolutely essential to learning and leadership development. In the next chapter, I describe how our programs sought to build Maine educators' capacity to learn from these sorts of information.

The stories I have excerpted in this book are largely success stories. They are examples I've chosen because they represent reflection that generated insights and learning. Not every participant in our programs, however, became adept at reflection through the cognitive, interpersonal, and intrapersonal lenses. They were not all successful at using the essential questions in Figure 7.1 to generate streams of evidence that could help them know their own performance talents and limitations.

It's fair to say that every learner in our programs found the process demanding. Some learners rely so heavily on cognitive models of learning that they struggle to see how the interpersonal and intrapersonal modes complement the cognitive. Some are so uncertain about their role and relationships at school that they never move past thinking of themselves, as one participant put it, as "only play-acting being a teacher leader." Many feel overwhelmed by the responsibility and the sheer complexity of leadership and struggle to frame their purpose and boundaries so they are manageable. Others struggle to attune themselves to the feelings and thoughts of others, to gain the level of "heedfulness" to others and to situational cues that is so necessary in school leadership (Spillane, 2006).

Given these hurdles, it is not surprising that our learners worked hard to open themselves to evidence of their own strengths and weaknesses and to ask, repeatedly, the core question: "How do I *know* I am leading?" It is risky business, business that requires a certain strength of conviction, a degree of self-assurance, and a great deal of support and active assistance from trusted colleagues and program staff.

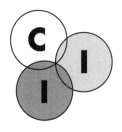

The Learning Environment for Leader Growth

WHEN I WAS A PRINCIPAL, a colleague once said that he learned more about his leadership from informal conversation with other principals than he did from his graduate program, conferences, or his supervisor. He was saying, I think, that he learned a lot about his own capacity to perform in his own school through reflection with experienced colleagues who had no immediate stake in his situation. They helped him see things in his performance that he alone could not see clearly and fashion options for action from them. Roland Barth (1997) has graced this form of learning with the term "craft knowledge." Robert Sternberg and Richard Horvath (1999) call it "tacit knowledge"—knowledge that we gain and use through informal channels, sometimes without being aware we are learning it.

The learning leaders in the preceding seven chapters have illustrated the many nonformal channels through which leadership learning happens. In this chapter I summarize the major elements of the learning environment that we have found in our programs to nurture learning. I take a step back from the learning itself and describe some conditions that help educators tap into their own capacities and cultivate new skills and knowledge than can immediately shape how they perform their craft.

We find four environmental conditions conducive to leader development:

1. Engagement in the practice of leadership
2. A plan to lead, a plan to learn, and a plan to reflect
3. Access to rich cognitive knowledge about learning and leadership
4. Partners-in-learning

Descriptions of our program practices are available online (www.portfolio
.umaine.edu/~edl).

MAKE LEADERSHIP PRACTICE THE SOURCE FOR LEARNING

We hear over and over from our participants that the deepest lessons result from efforts to apply a strategy, a technique, an idea, a suggestion in
their own leading. Whether we call it problem-based learning, learning-in-
action, or experiential learning, it is abundantly clear that it is through personal experience as leaders that most people come to understand whether
and how they can lead. Most adult learning theory substantiates this fundamental premise (Brookfield, 1995; Drago-Severson, 2004; Mezirow, 2000).

The difficulty lies in providing this important condition for leader
learning. How can a leadership development program create a curriculum
around adults' varying situations, personalities, and goals? These require
different experiences from one leader to the next. But they all require that
the learner understand how to use her or his work environment as a laboratory for learning. The first condition for leader learning requires that we
who are structuring programs view the leader's work environment as the
classroom, not our own classrooms or workshop settings.

The MSLN program was school based and work embedded. The master's
degree cohort program at the University of Maine follows that model as
well. The programs' activities, from the outset, engage participants in extensive diagnostic work to examine how their work environments functions and what the existing leadership norms and practices are. That is,
the object of study is each participant's particular organizational environment, the place where she or he aspires to lead. A heavy portion of the
cognitive curriculum—how teaching and learning occur, how schools
function and grow as organizations to support teaching and learning—
informs this line of inquiry throughout the program.

A second line of inquiry focuses on the leader her- or himself. As this
book amply illustrates, participants explore their interpersonal and intrapersonal capacities in the context of their growing understanding of the
leadership needs of their workplaces. Leadership Development Plans are
a formalized outcome of this exploration. They guide in a conscious way
the learning and the leading activities that constitute this performance
learning. It proceeds in an iterative manner (see Figure 8.1).

In this manner, the "leadership arena" where the learner is attempting to lead becomes "the classroom" or, as one of our participants labeled
it, "my laboratory." And the leader's "pebble in my shoe," arising from
the work in that arena, becomes the stimulus for learning. Our challenge

FIGURE 8.1. Elements of Performance Learning

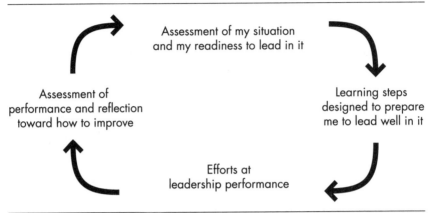

as program staff is to maintain this focus on "you, your leadership arena, and your goals for improvement." So the learning process is individualized and self-directed—an appropriate model for the learning of "lead learners" (Barth, 2001). In MSLN, staff members visited learners' schools routinely, often observing them in their leadership roles and sitting with them afterward to debrief. Similarly, program colleagues visited and observed one another. Program sessions, too, were held in members' schools.

The graduate cohort program at the University of Maine faced—and still faces—challenges making leaders' practice our classroom. We meet off campus in groups of 10–14, often in schools. We have developed an elaborate set of exercises for the study of students' schools and for their assessment of their own leadership readiness in their own schools. We find that students often come to us expecting to be relatively passive participants in the learning process; they, too, usually assume that learning will be largely cognitive. Our explicit emphasis on interpersonal and intrapersonal learning and on the reflective learning process described in Chapter 7 make the point early and often that learning will be active, focused on performance, and self-authored.

Another way that we bring experience to the learning process is through simulations and role-plays. In a variety of leadership situations we construct, participants learn to assess, strategize, and enact leadership. Most important, they have the opportunity in these relatively safe "fake situations" (which often turn out to be quite authentic once the interpersonal and intrapersonal dimensions "go live") to debrief, to "rewind the tape" to the point of a "critical event," and then to "replay it" using a different set of behaviors and ideas.

Making leaders' practice the classroom for leadership learning is enhanced immeasurably when school districts and leadership development programs collaborate. Districts support leadership development by embedding reflection and learning in the activities of leadership teams, supervision, and professional development. When graduate programs and professional development groups integrate their efforts with districts' school improvement and capacity-building efforts, everybody wins. As we found in MSLN, when superintendents invest in ongoing leadership development, they cultivate leadership talent *and* advance the performance of their students and schools.

HAVE A PLAN TO LEAD, A PLAN TO LEARN, AND A PLAN TO REFLECT

Leadership experience by itself is not enough to fuel learning. The environment must be planful and intentional. As Boyatzis, Cowen, and Kolb (1995) put it, "Experience does not necessarily equal learning. . . . People will not always make the best use of opportunities for development unless they are part of an intentional plan for development" (p. 76). So learning from experience and learning to perform differ. While experience is vital to what I call performance learning, it requires the structure of plans to shape the development of increasingly effective leader performance.

A second important condition for learning is captured in the Performance Learning Cycle (see Figure 8.2). Each of the learners in this book was expected to engage in the four activities in this cyclic process. Much of the curriculum of our programs is aimed at helping them to develop a deep and enactable understanding of these interacting activities. Taken together with the reflective-learning process (Figure 7.1), they are the means by which lessons can be extracted from experience and, presumably, made a part of each learner's growing capacity to lead. (This basic cyclic construct is explicated by Argyris, 1999; Boyatzis et al., 1995; Drago-Severson, 2004; Lambert et al., 1995; and Marnik, 1997.)

The *Plan to Lead* is based on the leader's assessment of her or his school—its goals and needs, its staff and their readiness to improve and to work together, and the history and norms of leadership that prevail there. We encourage our participants to read widely about teaching and learning, about organizational theory, and about school improvement to anchor their plans in a relevant knowledge base. Their plans to lead are often

FIGURE 8.2. The Performance Learning Cycle

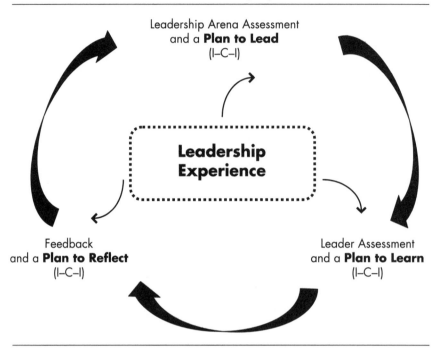

idealized and depict "how I want this to go." We ask our participants to identify in this plan some cognitive, interpersonal, and intrapersonal knowledge and skills that are necessary for success. And we ask that they be tailored to the specific realities of their school.

The *Plan to Learn*—the Leadership Development Plan—results from participants' assessment of themselves and their readiness to perform the leadership in the plan to lead. Goleman and colleagues (2002) describe this as the identification of gaps between the ideal (the plan to lead) and the real (the skills and capabilities I have to lead). I call this "finding a pebble in my shoe" to work on. Leaders then draw on the I-C-I framework to identify specific learning steps in each domain that they expect will prepare them to succeed at the plan to lead. (See Chapter 4 and the case of Nancy in this chapter.)

Feedback and reflection, as I describe them in Chapter 7, are essential means of making sense from experience. We find that reflective learning is far more productive when focused on a *specific* plan to lead and a *specific* plan to learn. Leadership experiences are so complex and multidimensional that they often feel overwhelming to the leader trying to make sense of them. A *Plan to Reflect* focused around three questions helps sort out that experience:

1. How did this go, compared to how I wanted it to go? (Did my plan to lead work?)
2. What did I do and how did my actions shape how it went? (Did my plan to learn prepare me well in this instance?)
3. What lessons emerge from questions 1 and 2 for my next plan to lead? My next plan to learn?

The plan to reflect includes ways to solicit feedback to inform answers to these questions and partners to help make sense of it. We help to structure ways that learners can solicit the perceptions of colleagues at school and colleagues and staff in our program. We have borrowed or developed an array of protocols for writing about experience, making sense of feedback, and orally analyzing experiences along the way. (See List of Resources.)

The value of the Performance Learning Cycle depends on the richness of the leadership experience it surrounds. Educators who come to us already playing leadership roles in their schools often are overwhelmed by the sheer amount and intensity of their experiences. Others, including those just beginning to consider leadership, do not have enough. They don't see themselves—and often are not—playing a leadership role yet. So they don't come to program sessions or respond to journal prompts with much of a story line to work from. We help them to negotiate a beginning role for themselves (even if it requires self-appointment as an informal teacher leader!).

Gaining insight through the cycle requires discipline and skill as well. The planning devices we use to structure the plan to lead, the plan to learn, and the plan to reflect are helpful to both the experienced and the novice leader. For the experienced leader, these frameworks provide a way to isolate one important pebble in one important arena of her or his work and to focus on improving practice through a Leadership Development Plan in that more manageable arena. For the novice, the plan to lead is a design for intervening in the life of the school in a new way—however tentatively. It serves as a strategy for dipping their toes in the leadership pool with the support of a learning plan alongside.

Enacting a leadership strategy generates feedback. Reflection generates adjustments to the plan to lead, giving the leader a better toehold on how to make a difference. Once they have become skilled at the learning process represented by the Performance Learning Cycle, teachers who aspire to administration can design new plans to lead and new plans to learn that incorporate goals and skills reflecting administrative leadership competencies. Those pursuing teacher leadership can hone the qualities needed in these vital roles.

Nancy, a young teacher in a K–3 school who hoped to become a principal, illustrates the Performance Learning Cycle in action. Her plan to lead involved mobilizing colleagues to use a new writing-instruction process. After 6 months of planning and implementation of the new writing process, Nancy's written reflections had documented "resistance" among some colleagues and timidity on the part of the principal. Here is her diagnosis of one leadership challenge—one pebble—she faced in this situation. It includes a goal she devised for improving her leadership:

> When someone confronts me I don't take the time to plan in any way at all. I seem to react to them immediately, emotionally, and in full force. I believe that if I can wait 5 seconds before even trying to respond, I may give myself time to see where they are really coming from. I may have a better understanding of what they are saying. It will also give me time to at least check in with myself to see what emotions may be just below the surface getting ready to explode.

Nancy's reflection turns the camera on both other participants and on herself. She examined the way her intrapersonal domain (her recognition of emotion and her ability to shape how that emotion affects her behaviors) was influencing her interpersonal domain (her ability to respond constructively to members of her faculty who raise questions or objections to the new writing process). She then identified a plan to lead in an improved way: Ideally, she wants to make every member of the team feel included so that they can remain open to understanding and learning the new approach to writing.

In addition, she has diagnosed her challenge, the pebble in her shoe: her natural tendencies that shut some people down and make them impervious or resistant to her influence. What, then, was her plan to learn? Nancy devised the following plan for her learning. It focused on changing three specific aspects of her interactive skill set:

- I will take 5 seconds before I respond to anyone about anything. During that time I will breathe deeply, and listen.
- I will be aware of my tone when speaking.

- I will watch for signs from the other person that my tone is too harsh (increased hostility in their body language, voice, on their faces, etc.).

Her Leadership Development Plan (LDP) identified leadership contexts where she planned to try these new behaviors and provided a time frame for her efforts to adopt them:

> I want to try this with everyone, not just with someone that I may be having a conflict with. I'm hoping this will help me to make this "check-in pause" a habit. . . . This is where I want to put my efforts for at least the next week. . . . I've looked at conflicts that I've been involved in, both successful and unsuccessful. It seems that I feel most successful in the ones that I initiate—when I go to someone else to work out a problem. I believe that is because I have learned to plan, or strategize, as well as anticipate and plan for possible outcomes.

Nancy's investment in a written LDP has helped her to define a very specific set of behaviors to work on. It took her a while to select "responding to hostile responses" and her affective and vocal "tone" from all the other possible learning goals. But her success as a learner was immeasurably enhanced because she could concentrate on learning new habits in these few, distinct intrapersonal and interpersonal patterns. She concluded her LDP with some specific steps to aid her learning, not merely her leadership action:

> I'm going to take a look at some videotapes of myself and perhaps do some audiotaping to begin identifying some of the tones that I use. Then I can build a repertoire of tones and have a choice of which I use, rather than have my tones choose my fate for me.

Nancy's LDP included a cognitive dimension addressing her proficiency with concepts and techniques from the writing-process curriculum. The issue, however, was not her expertise; she had taken courses and attended workshops. As an accomplished teacher who had used the process herself, her cognitive grasp was not a problem. Nancy struggled to understand how other teachers with less experience and perhaps less passion for the curriculum needed to learn it. Her cognitive goal was to learn from listening to her colleagues how the "content" could best be shared with them so they could not only learn it but see the value in it.

Over the course of a year, Nancy's plans to reflect engaged her in bi-weekly journal entries describing what she had done in her role as informal coordinator of the writing-process initiative, how her plans to interact differently with specific colleagues had worked, and what "tweaks" to her learning plan these required. She wrote more structured "critical incident" analyses on her performance in specific events where her LDP goals came into play. She shared her journals with a program staff member, who responded to them by e-mail and she brought journals and critical incident analyses to program meetings where they became the focus of discussion in a small colleague-critic group every month. Approximately every 6 weeks, Nancy and her colleagues were expected to revisit their LDPs and to adjust them so that their plans to learn became a living document reflecting their learning.

At the end of the year, Nancy's reflective portfolio narrative noted successful aspects of her performance and some challenges she would continue to face. She had "asked the staff to give me feedback regarding my leadership [and it made me feel successful as a leader that] they trusted me enough not only to fill out and return the survey, but several talked to me face to face, sharing their insights, providing me with valuable straight talk." She wrote:

> My intensity and energy is sometimes seen as aggressive and overwhelming. When I am involved in a project or discussion I have to work very hard to be sure that my verbal language and physical movement do not send the message that I can't slow down and bring them aboard. . . .
>
> Especially during confrontations, I "give away" what I'm feeling from moment to moment. This seems to cause others to react to my physical responses more than to my verbal comments. Even when I've said to another person, "I'm trying to understand your view," my facial expressions or crossed arms would quickly give away what I was feeling inside. I have allowed my body language to interfere with the open sharing of ideas.
>
> This is truly a challenge for me.

The Reflective Learning Cycle, for Nancy and many others, shows leaders how what they do and say shapes how those around them respond to the initiatives they put forward. Writing about the events and people in Nancy's leadership arena—including her own performance—helped to pin them down in time and space, to "diagnose" how she might behave differently "next time." And that pinned-down description gave her the opportunity to say, OK, now I can prepare myself to do this better by working on that aspect of my performance. Using the I-C-I framework helps to sort out these "aspects" and to more specifically identify behaviors, "tones," and knowledge bases that need work.

Learning doesn't come easy in the cognitively complex and often interpersonally messy world of school leadership. Without a plan to lead, it's almost impossible. Without a plan to learn, it's at best a random process. And without a plan to reflect, learning comes by sudden insight and unexpected epiphany rather than by systematic inquiry. As Karen Osterman (1998) put it, "On reflection, the [leadership] problem becomes a stimulus for learning, since the reflector is face to face with actions that are not consistent with values or are ineffective in reaching stated goals. This analysis can lead to new understanding and new strategies" (p. 11).

TAP A RICH ARRAY OF COGNITIVE KNOWLEDGE ABOUT LEARNING AND LEADERSHIP

The Performance Learning Cycle focuses our learners on their schools and their own performance. As we saw in Chapters 5 and 6, this process provokes a great deal of thought about the powerful interpersonal and intrapersonal dimensions of that experience. But the learner's success requires more than peering inward and examining relationships and interactions. It benefits greatly from two sorts of "outside supports": the knowledge base represented by relevant literature and colleagues who assist in the reflective process. In this section of the chapter, I offer a summation of the first of these and take up the second in the next sections.

What have we found to be the most helpful relevant literatures for our learning colleagues? How have we managed to build access points to them? We see ourselves as conduits to relevant literatures, not as experts; we transparently share the responsibility for the cognitive learning with every participant in each cohort and "deputize" each person to be a resource for all others. Given the richness of relevant literatures, the speed with which they multiply, and ready access through the Web, this works well. The ample sharing within our cohorts of "great articles," "super ideas," and "terrific books" is testimony to its value.

The assessment and planning frameworks of the programs—the planning to lead, learn, and reflect—define for participants and for us what literatures might be relevant. Armed with goals to make a difference for kids, an initiative to lead, and a diagnosis of "what I need to learn in order to be effective here," participants are motivated to find new cognitive knowledge to inform their own and their colleagues' efforts. The cognitive learning goals and steps of their LDPs specify classroom practices, management procedures, school change theories, facilitation methods, conflict-resolution processes, and the like. The cohort serves as a resource pool for each member to learn about such things. But the staff takes on a primary role, particularly at the beginning of the programs. We assign readings designed to open conduits to resources that will address learning needs as they emerge from the planning process.

We target two major literatures: one dealing with effective learning and teaching, the other with leadership and organizational change. A third literature—on adult learning—is important as well but plays a somewhat different part from the first two. In essence, these three literatures provide concepts, theories, analytic structures, and practical advice to our colleagues as they develop their plans to lead, create, and monitor their plans to learn, and make sense of their learning and leading through reflection. (See List of Resources.)

For example, in the domain of literature on learning and school improvement, we have used to good effect Linda Darling-Hammond's *The Right to Learn* (1997), Kathleen Cotton's (2000) summary of conditions for learning, Robert Sternberg's (2007) work on learning styles, Garmston and Wellman's (1997) and Charlotte Danielson's (1996) works on assessment and data-driven instruction, and materials from the school restructuring and reform movements such as those assembled through the Coalition for Essential Schools. With well-defined LDPs in hand, our participants can focus more specifically on alternative approaches to math instruction, on new frameworks for behavior management, or on case histories of successful strategies for engaging parents in school.

In the domain of literature on leadership, we draw from writers who present school leadership in the context of school improvement such as Roland Barth (1990); Michael Fullan (2003); Robert Evans (1996); Debbie Meier (2002); and Ken Leithwood, K. S. Louis, S. Anderson, and K. Wahlstrom (2004). These now include works from the growing literature on teacher leadership (Ackerman & Mackenzie, 2007; Katzenmeyer & Moller, 2001; Lieberman & Miller, 2001; and York-Barr & Duke, 2004). In addition, the broader literatures from business and on organizational change have proven helpful (Bolman & Deal, 2003; Goleman, Boyatzis et al., 2002; Heifetz, 1994; Senge, 1990).

Most helpful to participants' LDPs have been books and articles that identify specific leadership processes such as redirecting a group's discussion, intervening with an angry person, or active listening. These "leadership process" resources usually relate directly to interpersonal learning goals. Kegan and Lahey's *How the Way We Talk Can Change the Way We Work* (2001), Johnson and Johnson's *Joining Together* (1995), Rees's *How to Lead*

Work Teams (1991), and Isenhart and Spangle's *Collaborative Approaches to Resolving Conflict* (2000) are examples. The alternative leadership techniques that can be generated from such sources have often inspired new strategies for immediate adaptation and implementation.

The third field of literature that we draw on deals with adult learning. These are resources that can speak directly to the learning journey our colleagues have embarked on and can help them both understand how to make sense of their own past experience and to structure better their future reflection. Old standbys include Osterman and Kottkamp (1993), Barth (2001), Lambert et al. (1995), Argyris and Schön (1974) and our earlier work in the vein of this book (Donaldson & Marnik, 1995). More recently, resources have included protocols and structured activities to promote professional reflection and learning in schools. (See the following sections.)

We worry sometimes that we are not providing enough attention and access to cognitive sources of learning. Ethel, a talented teacher leader, remarked, "It's really the I-I that has made the difference for me. I can learn the C stuff anytime, but in my work with others, it's the I-I part that's been the most important." The greatest value in our leadership development program has been that it elevates the "I and I" and gives leaders some tools for learning in these dimensions. While the "C stuff" can be learned "anytime," we remind our learners that "C stuff," which is so important to their plans to lead, needs constantly to be mined and used.

PARTNERS-IN-LEARNING: THE LEARNING TEAM

Our programs have from the beginning followed collaborative learning principles, now popularized under the rubric of "professional learning communities" (DuFour, Eaker, & DuFour, 2005; Norris et al., 2002). Our participants, practically to a person, report that working alongside fellow learning leaders joined in a small learning collaborative was essential to their learning. Our programs seek to create this environmental condition by working in cohorts of 25–30, by forming small learning teams of 4–5, and by having staff work in one-to-one coaching roles. All three of these are purposefully structured as learning relationships around the goal of stimulating and supporting each member's leadership growth.

The cohort is the largest learning group; it is formalized as a community of learners with explicit norms to support group learning. Activities are facilitated by staff and focus largely on cognitive and interpersonal goals from leaders' Leadership Development Plans. The cohort is also the format in which staff discuss and facilitate learning structures such as diagnostic activities in the school, the plan to lead, the Leadership Development Plan, and formats for reflection. The cohort, as a whole, can mimic the behavior and affect of a school faculty and, in this respect, can serve as an excellent medium for role-plays and for reflections on group dynamics.

The third learning relationship—one-on-one coaching—will be taken up in the next section of this chapter. The second—the small reflective practice groups known as colleague-critic teams—is the subject of the remainder of this section. These are groups of 4–5 participants designed to include members as diverse as possible while maintaining geographic proximity so the team members can assemble easily and visit one another's schools. They usually include teachers and administrators, men and women, and educators from different grade levels. Where possible, we mix private and public school educators as well. Our programs have, on occasion, included two other leader types: school board members and parent leaders.

Colleague-critic teams (CCTs) exist for one purpose: to stimulate and support the learning of each member through what Ellie Drago-Severson (2004) calls "collegial inquiry." We structure team-forming and team-building activities as CCTs begin and continue them throughout their lifetimes. Each team generates its own written norms, learns to use reflective learning protocols, and supports each member's attempts to grow. When possible, CCT members visit one another's schools, often meeting in schools, and observe one another's leadership performances. They are essential vehicles for the Feedback and Reflection phase of the Reflective Learning Cycle (Figure 7.1) and dwell most on interpersonal and intrapersonal learning.

The CCT process is described in more detail in other documents (Donaldson, 1998; Donaldson & Marnik, 1995; Mackenzie & Marnik, 2006) and by other people (Drago-Severson, 2004; DuFour et al., 2005; National School Reform Faculty, 2005; Senge, 1990). One example will serve to illustrate the importance of two key qualities: the safety to share authentic learning challenges and experiences, and effective questioning. Staff take an active part in helping each CCT develop strong norms around safety and inquiry and these norms become a basis for periodic team self-assessment by the members. The two qualities and the norms that support them explain, in large part, a CCT's success at both stimulating and supporting leadership growth.

The following is a reconstructed account (adapted from Donaldson, 1998) of a CCT meeting in which I participated as a program faculty member. Peter (an elementary school principal), Sarah (a middle school teacher leader), and Sharon (a high school principal) constituted the team. In this excerpt, Sharon is at a crucial point in her efforts to refocus her LDP on a "pebble" that she now realizes has been chafing her foot for some time.

The four of us are seated around four student desks pulled together into a rectangle. Coffee mugs, chips, papers, and pens cover our space. Peter, Sarah, and I all lean forward on our elbows, intent on Sharon's words. It's late afternoon and we're at Peter's school for the monthly meeting of our colleague-critic team. Now, an hour into our session, it's Sharon's turn to consult with us about her new "pebble."

"My intrapersonal challenge is about being judgmental," Sharon begins. "I'm beginning to see this about myself: One of the reasons I stop listening to people in meetings is that I've decided they're uninformed, misguided, flat-out wrong. I'll be sitting in a meeting, trying to get people to at least agree on some common points, and someone will get on a soapbox and blabber. Inside my head, I'll be saying, Right! Sure! What the hell does he know about what he's talking about? Then I'll begin planning what I'll say next. . . . before he's even finished."

"Oh, my gosh, Sharon, I do the same thing!" Peter adds. "But what makes you turn off like this? What do you mean, 'judgmental'?"

Sharon ponders for a few seconds. "It's really very simple. Some people just don't know what they're talking about. They're uninformed about the kids we discuss or they blame the kids for their problems! Or they haven't prepared for the meeting. As soon as I see this, my mind just shuts down on them. They're wasting my time and probably everybody else's."

Sarah joins in with a question to Sharon. "So, you've identified this as your intrapersonal challenge. Why do you want to change this part of your leadership?"

"I guess from our discussions and reading I've seen how this type of behavior cuts me off from people I'm trying to lead. I mean, how can you be collaborative if you're not giving some people the time of day?"

Pete jumps back in. "Yeah, I know what you mean. I think I do the same thing sometimes. With some people on my faculty, I've gotten to the point where I prejudge them. I don't expect to get anything of quality from them even before they come to a committee meeting! That's not good."

"As a teacher, I know exactly what you mean," Sarah adds. "The last principal at my school used to do that a lot. It got so some of us stopped even trying to take part in some conversations."

Eagerly turning to Sharon, Peter asks, "So, Sharon, have you thought about what you can do about this? I mean, I face the same thing and can learn a thing or two here!"

From Peter's question, the conversation turns toward Sharon's LDP. She is considering adding an intrapersonal goal to learn to alert herself to when she is shutting down on a colleague. The CCT discusses her plan to gain control over her "judgmentalness" but presses further. One member makes the point that "there seem to be two parts to this: first making yourself aware that you're feeling judgmental; second, changing how you usually act toward them interpersonally."

Questions probe Sharon's thinking about how she can behave toward these "clueless colleagues" in such a way that they do not feel devalued but, instead, feel that their perspectives and feelings are important to the discussion. Sharon states, "I've learned that if I let my feelings show, I can make the meeting even worse. I mean, it doesn't help anything for me to blurt out something like, 'How did you come up with that?' It just creates hard feelings. As leaders, we're supposed to be trying to build consensus."

Sarah enters with a question for Sharon: "So, what do you think will help you in these situations? How will you meet this challenge?"

"Like I said, I'm going to work on patience and tolerance in meetings. . . . I'm going to try to use that little warning bell in my head that says, Don't turn him off." Sharon reviews the sheet of paper in front of her where she's sketched out her Leadership Development Plan. "I'm just going to try to control my impulse to judge, not to start composing my answer to someone before they've finished speaking. I'm going to work on my listening skills."

We all think about this for several moments. Then I ask, "That sounds like a good strategy for helping to keep the meeting positive. It would be good to get more specific about exactly what listening behaviors you can use in these situations. I mean, when your alarm bell goes off, how will you act differently toward these people than you usually do?"

"Yeah," Sarah says, "I was wondering that too. With our old principal, we knew instantaneously when he was shutting down. I'll bet some of these people on your staff know that too. How can your nonverbals tell them that you're actually hearing them?"

"I've been thinking about that, too," Sharon answers. "I haven't written anything out yet, but this is where my intra-personal goal and my interpersonal goal meet. I've got to dig out those articles about active listening and see if there's something I can use. When the alarm bell rings, I've got to be able to show the person I think is wrong that I'm still open to his view."

We discuss Sharon's need for new listening strategies. Members of the group make suggestions and ask further clarifying questions. Sarah even remarks on Sharon's attentiveness to people in our little group, saying, "I have a hard time picturing you doing this [judging and shutting out] at school." Sharon jots notes to herself on her LDP and concludes with a promise to herself to "journal" about these ideas and try one or two out in meetings in the coming 2 weeks.

Then the conversation takes a new turn, when Sarah asks, "But what are you going to do with your real feelings about these people? You seem to be stuffing them in a closet and I don't know if that's good for you."

I add, "Yeah, I was wondering about that too. Your plans sound good for the committee and the school, but if you're convinced that someone is wrong and concerned that their wrongheadedness might lead to something bad for the school or for a child, should you be sitting on those feelings?"

Sharon thinks this over. "I don't see that I have much of a choice. I've told you what happens sometimes when I speak out. I think I've got to try stuffing it."

Then Peter weighs in. "I don't know if it's an either-or. Have you thought about ways to express your disagreement with someone that might not shut them down? Or ways to turn what they've said back to the group so they can evaluate it?"

"I'm just not very good at that, Peter. I know what all that stuff about collaboration says, but it takes too much time and patience."

"Yeah, Sharon," I interject, "but if you just stuff your real feelings in a closet, it's going to eat away at you. You're still going to be ranting and raving on the way home from meetings. Usually, our judgments about people come out in other ways."

"I know, I know," Sharon says. "You guys are going to have to help me figure out ways to say these things. I can't live without speaking my mind. It's just that my usual old point-blank straight talk makes some people defensive."

Sharon's turn in her CCT meeting is about to end. In her half hour of consultation with Peter, Sarah, and me, she has grappled with a leadership challenge that lies at the center of her work as a principal: Can she remain interpersonally open to all her staff? The cost of not doing so is that she loses some of them; who, after all, is going to follow a leader who does not give them the time of day? She's making progress understanding herself as she interacts with staff; with her CCT's support and questioning, her interpersonal knowledge is growing.

Sharon is also uncovering the link between this interpersonal challenge and her own internal workings, her judgmental thoughts about a staff member and her feelings about them as members of the faculty. This intrapersonal knowledge, she is learning, shapes her interpersonal behavior in meetings. Until she devises ways to handle her judgmental thoughts about a teacher's ideas and her sometimes disdainful feelings about the teacher, she's going to find it difficult to be interpersonally open and professionally respectful toward that teacher. Her team has helped her acknowledge how she is contributing to her own challenges as a leader and, like so many of our participants, to consider new possibilities and a "third way" out of her polarized dilemma (Kidder, 2004).

Sharon's is the kind of exploration into leadership that we all strive for: It's frank, and it grapples with an active problem—a pebble that chafes daily, eroding her effectiveness and causing her to worry. The safety of her CCT has grown over many meetings. Its members have learned how probing and questioning their experiences can reveal new understandings of the challenges and new possibilities for their own growth. Most important, a strong CCT assures a leader of support. As Sharon herself says "[I know] that you guys [are] going to help me figure out ways to make the changes I need to make in my own performance."

In the summative evaluations of our programs, many participants cite the educative power of their CCTs. In the best sense, they become mini-hothouses for self-directed learning, helping each leader make sense of recent experiences and plan ahead for new, and hopefully more effective, leadership. Chris put it this way: "The colleague-critic team is the place where I can 'think out' the issues that are plaguing me. . . . I leave our [CCT] meetings feelings refreshed, focused, and enthusiastic about my work."

PARTNERS-IN-LEARNING: THE FACILITATOR AS COACH

Isabel summarized the value of partners:

The CCT and the facilitator's roles are crucial. For me, they have been my safe shelter. It has been a place to be as honest as I can about what I'm experiencing and to give and receive equally as honest feedback in a way that makes me feel supported and protected. I always write before and after these interactions as part of the process to further identify and clarify what's happening in my head and heart.

In MASL and MSLN, staff members are known as "facilitators." In our graduate program, we continue to be known as faculty, but we try to behave as facilitators. Whatever the nomenclature, our goal is to stimulate and support learning that has personal and professional significance to each participant. We construe our work as nurturing, self-directed or "self-authoring" learning in the best tradition of adult development (Boyatzis et al., 1995; Brookfield, 1995; Drago-Severson, 2004; Mezirow, 2000).

We wear several hats as facilitators. One puts us in the role of structuring the environment and the activities of cohort meetings, drawing on a curriculum organized around plans to lead, learn, and reflect. Here, we function as leaders of the cohort as a learning community. We straddle the fence between planning for the group and adapting our plans to where the group needs to go. We present guidelines, frameworks, skill sessions, and reading and action assignments with the recommendation that "this has helped others make progress; if it doesn't work for you, let's develop a substitute that does."

A second facilitator hat we wear is coaching CCTs. Successful CCTs don't just happen. They need cultivation as they move through stages of formation and, hopefully, become high-performing learning groups. Staff engage as "coaches on the side" for each CCT, particularly in the early phases. We also share with CCTs a regimen of protocols, readings, and assessment processes to help each CCT be as purposeful and effective as it can be. (See List of Resources.) We are, in effect, facilitating a strand of our program curriculum on healthy group process and group leadership skills. (Our graduate program includes a stand-alone experiential-learning course in "task group leadership" as well.)

Wearing the third facilitator hat, each facilitator and faculty member serves in a coaching role, one-on-one, with a group of 12–15 participants. This process is often credited by participants as having the most impact. In this role, our job is to get to know the participant and her or his school as well as we can, to read and respond to her or his reflective journal entries, evolving LDPs, and other diagnostic and assessment vehicles such as periodic portfolios. A number of recent resources describe how coaching can benefit leaders and the skills sets involved (Daresh, 2001; Ellison & Hayes, 2005; Garmston & Wellman, 1999; Mackenzie & Marnik, 2006).

In MSLN, we employed three full-time facilitators, and a large part of their work was to visit and observe participants in their schools. This aspect of the program created continuous focus and support for learning for each participant in much the same way that in-house executive coaching programs do in business. But it is expensive and proved difficult for us to sustain. Our graduate program seeks to create the same coaching relationships between faculty facilitators and students, but we seldom reach the intensity that comes from knowing well students' work environments and seeing students "performing live" there.

Excerpts from a facilitator's e-mail exchange with one participant illustrates how this coaching relationship and process can function. Patience was one of our full-time MSLN facilitators. She had come to know Vlade, a young elementary school teacher, as his coach and the facilitator of his CCT through the 1st year of the program. Before the 2nd year, Vlade took a team leader position at a middle school. He also was appointed co-chair, along with a principal of the district's Supervision Committee—a group established by the superintendent to make the formal evaluation system more supportive of professional growth. Vlade made his teacher leadership role on this committee the focus of his plan to lead and his plan to learn (LDP).

We join Patience and Vlade's e-mail interchange in the early fall. Vlade is feeling his way as a new staff member with team leader designation. Teachers on the Supervision Committee seem defensive and the administrators are clearly acting in charge. He writes, "Our last meeting was a disaster. It changed directions at least five times. By the end of the meeting, groups were sitting around 'wordsmithing' a book by Charlotte Danielson. . . . My section went well, but the reality is, I am just 'window-dressing.' I have no real power."

Vlade wonders how he can exercise positive influence. The only role he can carve out for himself in the early going is as "undercover question asker"—attempting to bring to the surface important issues and opportunities by asking questions of administrators and colleagues. He determines to "meet with the administrator 'in charge' and attempt to get him to reflect on the meeting and share his reflections with me. Risky! New learning: It is a lot easier to redirect a group of students than a group of administrators."

Patience's e-mail response has an optimistic tone. She offers Vlade several resources to read that pertain to his situation (Chapter 7 of Linda Darling-Hammond's *The Right to Learn*, 1997; Rob Evans's *The Human Side of School Change*, 1996). She concludes with a reference to Evans: "He's talking more about the dynamic tension between 'dictates from the central office' and 'teachers' feeling vulnerable and undermined.' That could be your LDP right there—[how to devise a role for yourself to mediate this tension]."

In the ensuing weeks, Vlade and Patience continue to exchange e-mails. Vlade asks if Patience can visit his school when the Supervision Committee is meeting so she can observe him facilitating the group with the principal. She agrees. But Vlade's principal then tells him that his part of the meeting is only to be a discussion lasting 10–15 minutes. "I had planned for 2 hours," Vlade writes. "Shared leadership is a wonderful concept in theory. I think that I made him nervous." Vlade is frustrated. He had planned his part of the meeting carefully, even inviting several colleagues to his house to give him some feedback on a rehearsal of it.

Patience responds: "That's too bad. It does sound like he's scared. Have you talked with [the superintendent] or would that make things worse? . . . Do you think most of [the teachers] just want the new evaluation system done—they don't care if it's meaningful or not? . . . Can you galvanize some forces on the committee? Is it worth it? I'm still available if you decide it would make sense for me to be there. I could always come and watch what's going on and then we could talk about it."

Vlade uses Patience's questions to assess both his commitment to the Supervision Committee's goal and his understanding of his potential to influence teacher and administrator members. In December, Vlade's redrafted LDP now focuses on establishing his own knowledge base and communication skills to assert the importance of instructional assessment skills in teacher evaluation. His objective has been shaped to some degree by the results of a conflict-style inventory we used that suggested that Vlade had a tendency to "accommodate" when faced with conflict. His LDP focused on a strategy to make him feel more confident so that he would behave more assertively:

Objective: To be able to be more assertive with teachers and administrators around assessment and evaluation. I want to avoid becoming withdrawn when colleagues don't agree with me, and avoid being intimidated by the hierarchy. Develop a deeper level of confidence around what I know.

Why is this important? Being more assertive will help me to better promote current research around assessment and evaluation [in my work with the Supervision Committee so that its products reflect best practice around assessment and evaluation].

Action steps:

1. Develop a clear set of beliefs around classroom assessment and how effective classroom assessment promotes learning.
2. Clearly communicate those beliefs in writing and orally.
3. Check for understanding: Were my beliefs clearly communicated to the audience with confidence?

Patience observed Vlade facilitating a committee meeting and shared both the notes she took at the meeting and some thoughts she had about the impact of Vlade's leadership. She is able to describe Vlade's manner and words at different points in the meeting and show how his leadership carried the group forward and where he seemed to withdraw when, as she put it, "the group was moving too far into [minutiae that you find pointless]." Patience also used a framework of facilitation behaviors from Garmston and Wellman's work (1999) to provide Vlade with a summary of his own performance.

Vlade wrote Patience the next day: "I have done lots of thinking about yesterday's meeting and still have a headache. . . . The majority of the people around the table really don't want to change the [evaluation] system. . . . There are many things that I could have done differently, but the problem is that I feel like I put myself at risk by doing so. If I righted the ship, I don't see how [the principal co-chair] doesn't take that as undermining him. This teacher leader model is really complicated. . . . The reality is that public education is failing kids not because 5% of teachers are crappy teachers. Every teacher, good and bad, needs to improve. . . . I need to be a leader with a title so that I can better define what the title means!"

After more consultations with Patience and some retooling of his LDP to make it "more pointed" toward practicing specific facilitation skills, Vlade felt equipped to risk being more assertive. Within a month of his feeling dispirited, he was writing to Patience, "Let's say that [the meeting of the committee yesterday] was a sharp contrast to the last meeting and this time there was no evidence of me 'bending' to the hierarchy. At one point, I would describe myself as using a very strong voice with [an assistant principal] who talks all the time about the effectiveness of the current system. I would describe it as an opportunity to show that I know what I am talking about and that I am passionate about this. Let's just say that several people were bug-eyed. More to come . . ."

In the same e-mail, he asked Patience if she would be willing to write a reference to support his application for an assistant principalship. Vlade's year as a teacher leader had convinced him that "undercover" leadership was too slow for him, too incremental for a system that was "failing" kids. He wanted—and was hired for—a job as "leader with a title" and has never looked back.

Vlade and Patience's interchanges revolve around the "pebbles" Vlade encounters as a leader. In many respects, their coaching relationship simply gives Vlade a receptive ear for spinning out his experiences so that he can weigh them and understand his own part in them. Patience's responses offer Vlade unquestioning support as a person and as a learner. Their central feature is, ironically, questioning: What was going on in so-and-so's head when . . . ? What was going on in your head when . . . ? Had you considered . . . ? What if you had . . . ?

Patience's observations of Vlade "in action," though, add an invaluable dimension to Vlade's growing knowledge of himself as a leader. Through her "outside eyes," he is able to gauge more directly how, as Ron Heifetz (1994) puts it, his own moves on the dance floor are affecting—and being affected by—the other dancers. Her suggestions of readings, too, helped Vlade to stretch his understanding of how his school functioned and how leadership could be conceived so that he could feel effective. In this sense, our facilitators' coaching has given leaders both information about themselves and about leadership that they could integrate into their next performance strategies.

THE CONDITION OF LEARNING CONDITIONS

The four conditions for leader learning described in this chapter—ongoing experience in leadership, a means to plan and reflect, access to ideas and techniques, and steadfast partners-in-learning—are often not present for school leaders. The exigencies of the work itself crowd out the time and energy for learning from experience. Professional development for leaders often comes at far-flung conferences, disembodied from the real "pebbles" that chafe in leaders' shoes. And it's often available only to administrators, as our system seems not to recognize how essential teacher leadership is to school quality.

University-based programs, too, are constrained by the culture and conditions on campus. We overrely on cognitive frameworks for understanding leadership and leader knowledge. These frameworks, of course, are more amenable to chunking into courses that professors can teach in the normal delivery structures of universities than are the interpersonal or intrapersonal domains. Further, they are what faculty have learned and are prepared to teach. Without the help of a supportive dean and of several off-campus organizations, we would not have had the great fortune to innovate free of these constraints.

We were also fortunate to find school districts where superintendents and principals understood how vital it was to invest in developing leadership talent. While this was not true in every participating district, our learners usually found that their own leaders supported their risk taking and appreciated their initiative. In many cases, our participants introduced learning activities from our programs to their colleagues at school, creating a gratifying ripple effect.

Walter F. Ulmer (1999), a retired military officer, writes:

> The keystone to a relevant, healthy profession is learning. There can be no organizational learning if individual learning is truncated. . . . Organizational learning involves an awareness of the need to learn, a model for learning and the creation of an environment that supports and rewards learning. Neither the civilian nor the military worlds typically have all three parts: awareness, model, and environment. (p. 71)

We have found that the I-C-I model for learning, embedded as it is in practice, has the potential to make a difference in schools both through the direct efforts of our learners and through enhancing the capacity for leader performance in everyone. But district leadership is essential to raising awareness of the vital role leaders' learning plays in making schools more effective. So, too, is it essential to creating and sustaining an environment of compassionate and constructively critical partners-in-learning.

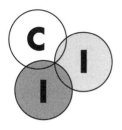

CHAPTER 9

Performance Learning

THE STORIES AND DESCRIPTIONS in this book have taught us a lot about how leaders learn to perform. We have confirmed what so many practitioners say: Cognitive knowledge is not enough to make a person a competent leader. But we've also learned that how we learn those vital competencies "beyond the cognitive"—the interpersonal and the intrapersonal—is complex and still rather mysterious.

Our Maine learners have taught us that these skills and sensitivities are learned through the performance of leadership activities in the company of plans and partners. Understanding how this works has challenged our old assumptions about leader preparation and propelled us toward new literatures. Professional performance is increasingly viewed as a sophisticated blend of, as Tom Serviovanni (2005) puts it, "head, heart, and hands." While historically we have represented leadership as "mostly head," teaching it through cognitive modes, we increasingly understand how the "hands and heart" shape both the leader's performance and knowledge.

We now see that leaders call on tacit knowledge as they work, particularly in the interpersonal and intrapersonal realms. We act and interact out of habit or style—and often not consciously. Leadership learning engages us in altering and adjusting existing tacit knowledge—a process of developing expertise that Robert Sternberg (1999) calls our "practical intelligence."

In this chapter, I summarize what we have discovered about performance learning and link our discoveries in each of the I-C-I domains to helpful research bases and literatures. Thus the chapter addresses what we know about how performance learning occurs and highlights some of the frontiers we need to be pursuing. The chapter concludes with a framework for designing leadership development opportunities that I hope will be helpful to leaders, the professional development community, and university faculty. (Resources we have found helpful in our work are described in the List of Resources, and a rubric for documenting learning is presented in the Appendix.)

The chapter begins with the cognitive domain, and then moves to the interpersonal, and finally to the intrapersonal. I summarize the types of knowledge encompassed within each domain, and then move to what we and others are learning about how that knowledge is acquired. To review, the three domains incorporate a total of seven core knowledge areas:

COGNITIVE DOMAIN

1. Instructional literacy
2. Organizational literacy

INTERPERSONAL DOMAIN

3. Relationship-building
4. Mobilization

INTRAPERSONAL DOMAIN

5. Philosophical platform
6. Self-awareness and self-management
7. Self-assessment and career choice

COGNITIVE LEARNING: BUILDING BLOCKS
FOR EDUCATIONAL DESIGN

The cognitive domain is the reserve for those facts, ideas, and systems of ideas that leaders can bring to decision making and planning to make schools high performing. Leaders in this book drew on an impressively broad array of such cognitive material: assessment procedures, models for science teaching and curriculum, theories of instructional effectiveness, strategic planning systems, and tactics for sharing decision making, to name a few. Two core knowledge areas lie within the cognitive domain: instructional literacy or knowledge about effective learning and teaching, and organizational literacy or knowledge about how schools as organizations function and improve.

With regard to *instructional literacy*, the heart of leadership work is about children and learning. It's about teaching and adults' capacity to provide what students need. Leaders need to have a strong working understanding of how children learn and how adults best teach so that their own performance can center on the school's core work. Since leadership is about mobilizing other adults to be as effective as they can be with children, leaders need to know enough about learning and teaching to ensure wise choices about classroom practices, curriculum planning, and professional conduct.

Instructional literacy permits leaders to link instructional issues in their schools to relevant research and theory and to develop with their colleagues strategies that can be supported by this knowledge base. Four major topics constitute the cognitive foundation of instructional literacy:

1. Intellectual, social, psychological, and moral development of children, particularly focusing on the age range that the leader's school serves;
2. Strategies and techniques teachers and other staff use to enhance student learning and development;
3. Strategies for planning and evaluating programs of instruction and development to support adults and children;
4. The nature of staff competencies in this work and how these can be assessed and cultivated.

Given the wide range of instructional issues leaders face—from the behavioral challenges faced by a single student, to aligning curriculum, to altering assessment and reporting systems, to ratcheting up teacher evaluation standards, to refocusing the purposes of co-curricular athletics programs—the leader's cognitive foundation for instructional literacy is an essential "entry key" to successful leadership.

The second core cognitive knowledge area is *organizational literacy*. Formally, we often refer to this as *organizational theory, change theory, management systems*, and the like. Practically, it's the foundation of knowledge that gives leaders a way to analyze how the school as a whole is working or not and to invent strategies for reshaping it into a more highly functioning organization. We identify four foundational topics within organizational literacy:

1. Understanding social, cultural, and political forces beyond the school and how they shape the constituencies and purposes of schools;

2. Diagnosing the school's structures and systems and their impact on children and adults;
3. Designing strategies to make the culture, structures, and systems of the school support more effective performance by adults and children;
4. Understanding relevant models that explain the role and function of leaders in schools.

Organizational literacy helps leaders and schools adapt to changing demands from outside and changing conditions inside the school. A strong knowledge base helps leaders to inform and facilitate wise choices about management, structure, and change processes.

What have we learned about how leaders gain these two important cognitive literacies? Three lessons have emerged from our work. First, traditional learning methods are useful, but their contributions to performance are quite limited. These methods can be described as "pre-service" or "before performance." They typically include readings, lectures, discussions, and writing and recall. Our participants tell us that much of this "is interesting and new," but as one person put it, "it's too much information for me to use. I don't know what to do with it all." Most knowledge imparted in this fashion is taken in through the neocortex and stored in forms that are rational, logical, and often inert. In these forms, such knowledge is not readily available to leaders unless they have the time to rummage around in the brain's filing system or refer to notes or a book. As helpful as it might be in providing thoughtful and accurate guidance to decisions, it's not particularly useful in performance situations.

A second form of cognitive learning, however, does bring facts, ideas, and theories to life in the leader's practice: targeted learning in response to a perceived need. When our participants found a pebble in their leader shoes and generated a plan to learn to address it, their motivation and focus as learners skyrocketed. Their LDPs gave them specific cognitive learning goals: to understand Charlotte Danielson's (1996) framework for instructional effectiveness; to be able to explain the hands-on methods for math instruction in the new curriculum; to summarize the benefits and liabilities of looping or of 4 × 4 block scheduling. This needs-based cognitive learning not only happened faster but also was put to use far more readily than generalized learning because the performance goals of the LDP gave it a context for implementation. Resources included books, articles, the Web, and the network of colleagues in our programs and at school.

A third form of cognitive learning was perhaps the most widespread: generating an accurate appraisal of practices and conditions within the school and its classrooms. Active leaders are busy becoming instructionally literate and organizationally literate about their own school! By far the heaviest learning activity for our learning leaders, as their stories illustrate, was in the conversations, meetings, observations, and strategy sessions with school and district staff, with students and parents, and in the halls and classrooms. At every turn, we encouraged them to blend this "data-based" knowledge base with the literature and ideas acquired through the first two methods. That is, the power of cognitive knowledge acquired from outside the school walls lies in how it can help leaders and others make sense of knowledge acquired within those walls.

These three methods of cognitive learning become increasingly embedded in performance. We find that all three are worth encouraging. We also find that, with new recruits to our program, the predominant expectation is that they will learn from us and from books—the traditional way. Consequently, we structure explicit ways to facilitate learning in the more self-directed paths described in the second two methods. Self-directed-learning models represent a superb ideal for schools as learning organizations—and particularly for their "lead learners" (Boyatzis et al., 1995; Brookfield, 1995; Mezirow, 2000). They involve the disciplined use of the Reflective Learning Cycle and the conditions I outline in Chapter 8. We find, given these conditions, that leaders are hungry for good research and sound theory and consume well-presented professional knowledge ravenously.

Becoming instructionally and organizationally literate is all about eliciting, locating, sharing, and applying cognitive knowledge appropriately. Leaders cannot know all that needs to be known in every situation they meet (indeed, some would say they cannot know it all in *any* situation they meet!). Even then, there's a whole lot more to leadership expertise than simply knowing. Leaders' success hangs more on how they facilitate the use of cognitive knowledge among others—which brings us to the second dimension of leadership knowledge: the interpersonal.

INTERPERSONAL LEARNING: IN AND FROM PERFORMANCE

The stories in this book highlight the significance of interpersonal challenges to leaders and to their success at mobilizing others. Questions abound about "my effectiveness" at conveying a difficult message to a reluctant teacher, at facilitating a heated discussion in a team meeting, at offering heartfelt appreciation to colleagues for work well done, at asserting the school's needs to the central office, or at simply listening attentively to an upset child or angry parent.

Chapter 5 explored the territory of interpersonal learning and provided a detailed summary of the interpersonal skill sets: forming solid working relationships, monitoring interactional and situational cues, intervening to mobilize, monitoring individual and group relationships, and self-monitoring. These are truly performance competencies: These skills show up in performance situations; outside those situations, they're latent. Because they have this in-performance nature, we find that these skills can best be learned in and from performance.

What do we know about how this interpersonal learning process happens within us? How do we draw from a leadership experience lessons that help us, the next time, be more aware of others' viewpoints and feelings, facilitate consensus more skillfully, or assert an argument more clearly without shutting down doubters? A growing literature linking our social, emotional, and relational qualities to organizational effectiveness and leader success offers us some guidance.

This research delves into interpersonal sensitivity (Hall & Bernieri, 2001), how social skills develop (Boyatzis et al., 1995), and into the nature of emotional and social intelligence (Goleman, 1995, 2006). Brain research reveals the vital influences of emotion in shaping how we work and live with one another. We are connected emotionally through "open loops" to one another, "regulated" by one another's feelings and by the existence or absence of "limbic synchrony" and "limbic resonance" (Lewis et al., 2000). Despite our hopes to the contrary, *how we work together and what we can do together are not largely decided by reason but by the emotional and social chemistry that leaders help to cultivate.*

Daniel Goleman (2006) stresses that effective leaders draw on "the full panoply of social intelligence . . . from sensing how people feel and why, to interacting smoothly enough to move people into a positive state" (p. 280). He describes the in-action nature of interpersonal knowledge, emphasizing that it relies heavily on our "'non-cognitive' aptitudes—the talent, for instance, that lets a sensitive nurse calm a crying toddler with just the right reassuring touch, without having to think for a moment about what to do" (p. 83).

Developing expertise in relationship building and in mobilizing others to action, the two core interpersonal knowledge areas, focused many of our participants on specific skills and abilities in specific situations. Goleman captures a number of these in his concept of "social intelligence":

- empathy (the ability to sense how others are feeling);
- attunement (the ability to pay attention to emotional cues in situations);
- social cognition (knowledge of how the social world works, what motivates behavior and shapes interactions);
- synchrony (the ability to "read nonverbal cues instantaneously and act on them smoothly");

- self-presentation and influence (the ability to behave in purposeful ways to shape how interactions progress to a desired end) (pp. 86–97).

These and other relational skills and dispositions related to leaders' capacity to build trust (Bryk & Schneider, 2002; Tschannen-Moran, 2004) and to generate collective action or "co-performance" (Spillane, 2006) are now widely viewed as essentials for successful leadership.

Researchers are exploring how the nonrational functions of our brains are involved in patterning these interpersonal skills and abilities. Brain research demonstrates that we process much of the information and emotion of interpersonal events unconsciously (located in the amygdala and hippocampus, not the neocortex) (Goleman, 2006; Lewis et al., 2000). We process emotional and social cues through a sort of autopilot that we've developed since childhood. Our responses to those cues—our facial expressions, words, tone, body language—are largely patterned by our past experiences and personality. Our ability to function in our professional environments, as elsewhere, emerges from our experience as we develop expertise with people and tasks. Robert Sternberg and his colleagues have explored this learning process, calling it our "practical intelligence" as leaders (Sternberg et al., 2000).

How, then, do we change our interpersonal patterns? How do we learn to alter the tacit knowledge that guides how we act with and react to people in leadership situations? The interpersonal learning process engages us in three stages: becoming aware of how we currently function, understanding what a better way to function might be, and developing through practice new skills and patterns of behavior that more closely match this better way. Richard Boyatzis and colleagues (1995; Goleman et al., 2002) describe this process as a matter of "five discoveries." Discoveries 1 and 2 "get you motivated to change" and 3 through 5 are "how change happens" (Goleman et al., 2002, p. 138):

1. Clarifying my ideal self: Who do I want to be as a leader?
2. Clarifying my real self: Who am I as a leader?
3. Developing a learning agenda: What strengths and gaps appear between my ideal and real leader selves? How can I build on strengths and address gaps?
4. Experimenting with new behaviors, thinking patterns, and feelings
5. Practicing the new behaviors and generating new neural pathways around successful behaviors, to the point of mastery

The LDPs our participants created from their plans to lead and our programs' practice-feedback-reflection processes follow this same logic. The

experiences of our participants reinforce the power of examining performance as the starting place for learning. As this literature indicates, our
ways of behaving, thinking, and feeling in leadership situations are often
not fully known to us. They are the result of a lifetime of developing "behavior sequences" that make us feel comfortable in social situations
(Goleman et al., 2002). By examining ourselves in situations where we
are attempting to lead, we learn how well these patterns match what we
seek to be doing as leaders (the ideal-real contrast).

Most educators who find themselves in leadership positions draw on
intuition and what Bruce Torff (1999) calls "folk psychology" which he
defines as "uncritically held beliefs" usually derived from experience and
the advice of respected colleagues (p. 196). Intuitive knowledge has four
qualities: It is powerful; it is hidden from view; it is "sometimes oversim-
plified, misleading, or inaccurate"; and it "often persists despite efforts to
improve or replace" it (p. 197). While much tacitly held knowledge is productive and useful in new situations, Torff and others concur with Boyatzis
that reflection on experience to reveal what aspects of "how I'm doing
things" work and what aspects seem not to work is vital to effective leader
performance and learning. Sternberg (1999) describes this learning process as "making the tacit explicit" (in Sternberg and Horvath, 1999,
p. 231). Kathleen, in Chapter 6, described it as moving from *unconscious*
competence or incompetence to *conscious* incompetence and then, in the
best of all worlds, to *conscious* competence.

Most leaders, in our experience, have little trouble *identifying better ways
to interact*—the ideals laid out in their LDPs. Our cognitive learning channels are full of such ideals from the literature on effective leadership. But
the most powerful sources are leaders' own intuition, supported by the
advice and counsel of colleagues within our programs. If they feel safe and
supported and can look closely at the way others are relating to them at
school, most leaders can locate the reticent team member, the habitually
in-conflict colleagues, or the footdraggers. Plans to learn begin to revolve
around acquiring such skills as active listening, using restatement in conflict situations, checking for understanding, mediation, and straight talk.
The real learning for leaders, however, comes in the effort to fold these
new behavior sequences into their own live performance.

Our Maine colleagues reinforce *the importance of experimentation and
practice in making this transfer.* Leslie Zebrowitz (2001) concludes her review of research on interpersonal sensitivity by stating that these skills
"develop through increasing interpersonal experience that provides feedback that contributes to implicit knowledge of [how to accurately assess
another person's feelings, thoughts, and motives]" (p. 342). Simulations
and role-plays bring "live interpersonal action" into the learning spaces of
our program sessions and offer powerful opportunities to act, obtain feed-

back, and reflect. Rehearsal and practice of specific techniques and skills called for in the LDP, carried out within the safety of our cohorts and CCTs, helps. The conditions outlined in Chapter 8 are essential in this process: specific learning goals, a plan to learn them, partner-coaches, and a learning group with strong norms to support experimentation and permit vulnerability. Goleman and colleagues (2002) maintain that

> experimentation with more positive alternatives is crucial. The new way of thinking, feeling or acting feels unnatural at first, something like putting on someone else's clothes. . . . [Without opportunities to try and to learn how a new interpersonal approach works, leaders] short themselves on learning to lead better. Often a leader will try a new approach once or twice, and then apply it—without giving himself the chance to *practice* it. (p. 157; emphasis in original)

Finally, the spirit of experimentation helps leaders *to transfer new habits and skills into "real" performance at school,* providing the litmus test so vital to authentic learning. Here, we find that facilitators and colleagues are essential, both encouraging the effort and structuring feedback and reflection on these critical new efforts. Behaving in a new way at work can provoke sidelong glances and questioning stares from others, and it does feel unnatural both to the leader and to others. Interpersonal knowledge grows most from unpacking our own experiences in trying to facilitate, manage conflict, and communicate. Without mechanisms for feedback and reflection, practicing new interpersonal skills can go for naught. Without the encouragement and support of fellow learners, the risks of changing can be so great that putting new skills to work *at work* will never be attempted.

Over time, most participants grow more proficient at understanding how leadership relationships work and what their own particular interpersonal challenges are. Their grasp of their own abilities to act productively in different situations grows, aided by sustained practice at understanding the tacit ways that they tend to act and improving skills and behavior patterns. We find, however, that interpersonal learning—learning that truly results in more effective ways of relationship building and mobilizing others—involves substantial doses of intrapersonal learning. Our ability to change our ways of interacting depend on our capacities for self-awareness, self-assessment, and self-management.

INTRAPERSONAL LEARNING: THE HEART OF THE JOURNEY

Learning leadership, Etienne Wenger and others have noted, involves a shift in identity (Wenger, 1999; Buck, 1993). Educators come to our programs seeking a new role or a new means of influencing events and outcomes. As they learn more about how leadership works, they begin to address how they can make their behaviors, self-presentation, and impacts match what they understand to be effective leadership. So leadership learning, as so many of our participants are fond of saying, "is about me": learning new ways to think, behave, and be that incorporate cognitive and interpersonal knowledge to "make me the best leader I can be in this school."

As Chapter 6 illustrates, educators freshly pursuing roles as leaders experience, in many instances, greater self-consciousness and often self-doubt because they are discovering that leadership changes relationships and places them in new roles. As they come to understand what it takes to lead, they wonder, Do I know enough to do this? Will I lose the comradeship of my teacher colleagues? Do I have the right to judge another person's competence? To force them to change? This "self-with-self" reflection, we have found, is a vital and rich springboard for intrapersonal learning.

It is largely through feedback and reflection that leaders gain an understanding of who they are as leaders. Essential to this learning is their ability to accurately assess their own assets and liabilities and to see how these are a fit for the leadership roles they choose to take on. As Nora and others demonstrate in Chapter 6, the goal of intrapersonal learning is to attain a "good enough fit" with the needs of the program, the team, or the school so that one's leadership is productive and sustainable for both the leader and the school.

What do we know about this intrapersonal learning process? We know that it requires developing the abilities to self-monitor and self-manage. These, in turn, require a degree of self-awareness: to see yourself as others see you (your interpersonal self) and to be honest with yourself about your own feelings, thoughts, and qualities (your intrapersonal self). As learners identify some leadership behaviors and qualities that they aspire to add to their own repertoires, they compare these with what they know of themselves. As they work to bring their own performance closer to the ideal, their skills of self-monitoring help them know how it's going. Their skills of self-management help them redirect their behaviors so that their performance moves closer to that ideal.

This is the heart of leadership learning. It is where the lessons from the cognitive and interpersonal domains integrate into a whole with the leader's self-understanding, morphing into new ways of performing that, presumably, result in mobilizing others. This integration draws on the following learning components:

1. Clarified statements of their ideals: What I believe about leadership for schools where all children learn (philosophical platforms);

2. Accurate understanding of their feelings, thoughts, and behaviors while in the action of leading (self-monitoring);
3. The capacity to alter performance so that "my walk more closely matches my talk" (self-management);
4. Accurate holistic assessment of leadership assets and liabilities and negotiating leadership roles that are productive and sustainable for both me and the school or group I serve (self-assessment and career choices).

These are the grist of the ongoing reflection that keeps alive the prospects for growth toward a leadership role that matches each aspiring leader's capacities. In the best spirit of self-directed learning, this leader is the author of her or his own intrapersonal journey. I will briefly summarize some of the lessons we've learned about these components.

Clarifying ideals sets the learner's sights. We formalize this by asking learners to write a series of leadership platforms about essential questions. The assumption is that leaders have values and beliefs that influence how they perform and that they need to be able to share them, defend them, and view them with a critical eye. A developed platform generates a concrete statement of "what I stand for" as a touchstone for their practice. Platforms are rooted in beliefs and values that frequently are very personal and often taken for granted. They focus on issues that are central to the effectiveness and leadership of schools:

1. What constitutes a well-educated child and how does she or he become one;
2. What constitutes effective teaching and learning, both in learning situations such as classrooms and in the general practices and culture of the school;
3. What constitutes an effective, self-improving school organization and what the role of the leader is in it;
4. What constitutes strong working relationships and what is needed to sustain them;
5. What constitutes a self-improving, "mobilized" staff group and what is the leader's role in "influencing others," particularly with respect to the use of power and authority.

As participants write their platforms and supply justification for them, they draw on their cognitive knowledge base, but they also reach back into their beliefs about how children grow, what productive behavior and citizenship look like, what makes for a healthy environment for children and adults, and what right any person has to exercise authority or wield power over others.

Learning "what I believe" and to articulate it well is an iterative process of drafting statements of belief, each with a succinct rationale that makes logical reference to knowledge bases that justify the statement. These draft platforms then are read widely by colleagues and staff, with feedback about clarity of meaning and the strength of the rationales. These send the authors in search of their own clarity of meaning and in search of stronger support—and often to a revision of the core statement itself so that it is more defensible and more articulate. (See also Lambert et al., 1995; Norris et al., 2002; Osterman & Kottkamp, 1993.)

This learning process requires disciplined thinking about "what I believe is right" and about "why I believe this is right" for students, the school, and leadership. Although never finalized, platforms establish ideals that then guide leaders' performance, literally becoming core principles for their plans to lead. In this respect, they are essential to leaders' learning goals; they are the talk that these learners seek to walk in their performance of leadership. In the gaps between talk and walk, these learners discover the pebbles in their shoes, the springboards for their plans to learn.

Self-monitoring and self-management, the next two components of intrapersonal learning, work synergistically. Knowledge emerges from leaders' learning to recognize the feelings, thoughts, and behaviors that arise in themselves. *And it involves cultivating an understanding of how to use this knowledge to deploy themselves* in leadership situations in a wise and productive manner. The interplay of monitoring and managing oneself in performance determines a leader's ability grow more effective in practice.

A word about what is monitored and what is managed: We encourage our participants to focus on their behaviors, thoughts, and feelings— three elements of themselves they can reflect on as they perform leadership. Most can readily recall behaviors: "what I did first, then how I responded to Esther, what I said next." But it's more difficult to retrieve thoughts: "what I was thinking when I did that" or "why I did that next." Curiously, it's often not so difficult to remember feelings, but it can be difficult (especially for men, we find) to comfortably articulate these: "I was feeling very intimidated then," or "When he said this, I just started to seethe inside."

Chris Argyris (1999) and Daniel Goleman (1995, 2006; Goleman et al., 2002) tell us that feelings are extraordinarily powerful influences on our both thoughts and behaviors in leadership. We often ascribe motives to other people based on how we perceive them or feel toward them. Our own emotional makeup triggers responses to people and situations that can, as Goleman puts it, "highjack" our thoughtful participation. So learning in this regard needs to focus leaders on understanding more fully how their emotional buttons influence their thinking and their behaviors in leadership situations (Neisser, 1993).

As they become more aware of how their interactions are shaped by internal and external stimuli, leaders gain a degree of self-management; they gradually come to determine their own leadership performance. We encourage participants to use self-talk as a means of coaching themselves to assert a new behavior pattern in interactions or meetings, to seal off impulses that are viewed as destructive, and to devote time and attention to preparing for leadership events and to self-care. (See Ackerman & Maslin-Ostrowski, 2002; Covey, 1991; Goleman, 1998a, 1998b; Goleman et al., 2002; Sternberg & Horvath, 1999.)

How does learning occur in this vital realm? The development of self-awareness, self-monitoring, and self-management is a young field. In our programs, relentless attention to self-study plays an important role in this learning by setting the expectation that self-knowledge and being intentional are prerequisites to effective leadership. We structure readings and discussion about the role of the intrapersonal domain and require self-monitoring and self-management strategies as part of leadership development plans. Nothing, however, can substitute for the power of feedback and reflection.

Feedback from others and from oneself are essential to self-awareness. Sources include personality, interaction, and leadership-style inventories. Structured protocols for reflecting on and in action give leaders a way to systematically examine their intrapersonal realities. They find that scripting "critical events" from their practice and replaying what they said, how they felt, and what they were thinking helps them to parse from the complexity of a situation how their own behaviors were shaped. Less structured reflective writing following leadership events is helpful, especially when shared with colleagues in the manner illustrated by the CCT and by Patience and Vlade in Chapter 8. Soliciting feedback on behavior and style from colleagues can show how others were experiencing a leader's facial expressions, words, actions, and moods. These provide grist for the "self-with-self" reflection that can help leaders reconcile differences between the leader's perceived self (Neisser, 1993) and the person that others experience.

In the move from self-awareness to self-management, these insights need a vehicle such as the LDP if they are to be incorporated into daily leadership performance. The plan to learn externalizes the leader's internal aspiration to behave in a new and, hopefully, more effective manner. Actually integrating a new pattern of behaving with others in a meeting or in daily interactions takes, as Goleman and colleagues (2002) put it, "practice, practice, and more practice" (p. 103). And that practice needs to be interspersed with reflection, reflection, and more reflection, not simply alone but with supportive—and critically thinking—peers.

The third core knowledge area in the intrapersonal domain is the leader's *holistic grasp of her assets and liabilities and her assessment of the fit with her leadership situation*. Learning activities, here, force leaders to step back, look at their career development on a broader scale, and assess what Peter Vaill (1989) calls the "envelope of optimal realism" (p. 134): knowing how I can contribute as a leader and what kinds of conditions I need to be "optimal."

Knowledge in this area can be seen as a running self-assessment. Experience, skills and type instruments, feedback from others, and self-monitoring yield an accumulation of observations about what a leader can do well, what a leader's natural tendencies are, and where her or his blind spots are. The accumulation of this "data" through reflection and the use of a rubric keyed to the seven knowledge areas described in this chapter generate a running catalog for the leader. We ask participants to "take stock" of this catalog every 3–4 months and to assemble a leadership portfolio every 12 months that presents her or his own self-assessment and assessment by others of assets and liabilities in these seven areas (see Appendix).

In Chapter 6 I described Nora's decision to step down from her principal position to more happily (and, she believed, successfully) serve as a teacher leader in her building. Nora's writing displays the more subjective and holistic meaning making of this last aspect of intrapersonal knowledge. It involves careful consideration of the "catalog" of leader assets and liabilities but in the context of bigger personal and professional considerations. Here, the lens turns away from asking only, What can I bring to the school? and includes, Am I the best person to do this? and, most important, Is this healthy and sustainable for me and my personal life?

These three essential questions help our leader colleagues to remain centered on why they have embarked on their learning journeys. They prompt evaluation not only of themselves but also of their home and personal ties and of the general healthfulness of their schools and districts as places in which to work and to lead. Taking stock of what many participants term the "balance" between the professional and the personal, they are synthesizing from their entire experience some intrapersonal observations that help them choose how to commit themselves to leadership work.

As this book has illustrated, they draw from many sources—how-to books such as Stephen Covey's *Seven Habits of Highly Effective People* (1989), autobiographical works that elucidate the personal side of leadership such as Roland Barth's writings, and the examples of leaders around them. We provide—and our participants find—works on professional learning that help them understand more fully their own learning styles and process requirements. (See, for example, Boyatzis, Stubbs, & Taylor, 2002; Drago-Severson, 2004; Lambert et al., 1995; Palmer, 1997.) Protocols help them explore core questions about their choices. (See, for example, the "onion model" in Korthagen & Vasalos, 2005.)

We find, however, that we need to insist on importance of periodic taking-stock activities, because the world often doesn't encourage them on its own. Reflective writing that basically focuses on the three questions above is, we think, essential. And when leaders' writing is shared around colleague-critic groups and with staff, they have the opportunity to hear others' observations on their "readiness" to lead and where the best fit is for them in a leadership role. Here is where the grand view of each leader's cognitive, interpersonal, and intrapersonal talents can find some measure of clarity and inform the leader's commitment or recommitment to leading.

THE LANDSCAPE OF LEADER LEARNING

Our experience inventing (and reinventing) our programs has taught us a great deal about how leaders learn. We knew, largely from our own experience as educators, that learning to perform teaching or leadership couldn't be done solely through cognitive channels. We knew from our own deeper conversations as teachers and administrators that these conversations themselves made us more conscious of our own craft knowledge and the gaps within it. But we didn't know much about how that worked. And we didn't know much until we created the Maine Academy for School Leaders in 1991 about how to encourage and guide that kind of learning.

We quite literally stumbled upon the interpersonal and the intrapersonal by listening to our participants and by looking for ways to represent the important "stuff" they needed to talk about and understand better. By listening a lot, by crafting journal prompts, by finding writers who wrote about these two domains, and by creating leadership development plans and the Reflective Learning Cycle, we gradually developed a curriculum for learning in the interpersonal and intrapersonal domains to complement the well-traveled curriculum of the cognitive domain.

Figure 9.1, The Landscape of Leader Learning, offers a framework for leadership developers to understand the intersections between what leaders need to learn and how they best might learn it. It also offers leaders a way to frame their learning choices as they engage in their own growth.

FIGURE 9.1. The Landscape of Leader Learning: Program Design Considerations

LEADERSHIP DIMENSION	LEADER'S DEVELOPMENTAL NEEDS DERIVE FROM:	LEADER'S SET LEARNING GOALS BY DIAGNOSING:	LEARNING MODE	TYPICAL LEARNING ACTIVITIES	PROGRAM ACTIVITIES
C **COGNITIVE**	*School Improvement* • Assessment of learning activities/outcomes • Teaching methods • Curriculum/program • Organizational change, restructuring, reculturing	*Knowledge of School Performance* • Best practices with students • Curriculum/programs • Organizational models for effectiveness and change • Leadership models	*Tell and Absorb (for the HEAD)* • Presentations • Reading (books, articles, memos) • Study groups • Other direct transmission of intellectual content	• Listen • Read • See demonstrated • Analyze and discuss • Reflect and write • Plan	• Speakers • Readings • Visiting schools/ sharing what works • Videos • Discussion/study groups • Analytical writing
I **INTER-PERSONAL**	*Relationship Development/ Mobilization Among:* • Me • Faculty • Students • Parents and public • The school district	*Human Growth Needs* • Our readiness to work together: relationships and skill levels • My relationships with others • My skill levels in relationship-building and mobilization • Climate and culture	*Show, Do, and Practice (for the HANDS)* • Demonstration and practice • Modeling • Experimentation and practice • Mentoring/coaching • Reflection on feedback on performance	• Feedback on performance • Practice, practice, practice • Skill training (e.g., listening) • Group process training • Role-playing • Co-learning with colleagues at work	• Performance-based learning in school • With coaching, mentors, support • Simulations/role plays • Skills assessment and development • Feedback training • Collaborative learning
I **INTRA-PERSONAL**	*Self-Development* • Knowledge of my talents, skills, foibles • Ability to read myself accurately • Ability to adjust my own performance • Clarity of beliefs and values • Self-confidence	*My inner self as I act as a leader and educator* • My fit with this leader role • Emotional health • Physical health • Balance in my life • Philosophical comfort/ clarity about the work	*Reflect and Understand (for the HEART)* • Stepping back, getting on the balcony • Contemplation of my own part in this • Adjusting my own part in this • Synthesis in a new understanding	• Reflection on feedback • Attuning to my feelings and my fit with the role • Assessing my assets and liabilities clearly • Clarifying core beliefs and values	• Reflective reading • Self-assessment inventories • Journaling • Writing leadership platforms • Exercise/stress reduction • Developing support network • Mentoring/coaching

Note: Adapted from "Inner Voice Tells Teachers How to Grow," by Gordon Donaldson, Summer 2004, *Journal of Staff Development.* Copyright © 2004 by National Staff Development Council. Adapted with permission of the National Staff Development Council, www.nsdc.org, 2007. All rights reserved.

Whether designing a program or drawing on the Landscape for individual guidance, this framework reminds us that leader learning begins with the learner's needs (Column 1), progresses to the learner's goals (Column 2), and then to designing learning activities (Columns 4 and 5) sensitive to the learner's learning mode (Column 3). In our programs, needs and goals emanate from the leader's plan to lead and the diagnosis of "pebbles" encountered in that practice. Learning activities and modes are identified in the "learning steps" of the LDP.

In this chapter I have emphasized the distinct character of learning in each of the three domains. But the Landscape reminds us that different types of leader knowledge require different modes of learning. Acquiring information through cognitive channels works for ideas, theories, management plans, laws, research results, and facts. But for interpersonal attunement, facilitating consensus, addressing conflict, or clear and effective speaking, only self-assessment, experimentation, feedback, and "practice, practice, practice" will do. And for a clearer self-awareness, more adept self-management, and more accurate holistic assessment, courageous self-observation, solicitation of feedback, and reflection are called for.

The Landscape's most profound message is the multimodal, self-authoring nature of leadership learning. Column 3 cannot do justice to the subtleties we see in our colleagues' learning—the ways that, for example, writing a critical reflection on a recent experience is clarified by a chapter from Rob Evans's *The Human Side of School Change* (1996) or that queries from colleague-critics generate a new way to approach the next leadership situation at school.

What makes leader learning most profound is the chemistry among the three domains. In the live action of performance, the three domains function synergistically and simultaneously. As Shirley's example in Chapter 1 illustrates, busy school leaders are constantly interacting with other people; these interactions are about educational issues and activities; and they call on leaders to monitor themselves—their words, feelings, and behaviors—to guide their effectiveness. Shirley's capacity for self-awareness and self-management are essential to helping her adjust her behaviors and manner with her colleagues in order to reach a goal that will improve learning. Learning to lead better is ultimately about how leaders synthesize their knowledge and skills in the three knowledge domains, a task that requires them to embrace three quite distinct modes of learning.

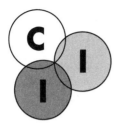

What We
Need to Do

THE PERFORMANCE LEARNING model introduced in this book enhances not only individual leaders' competencies but the success of their schools as well. When learning is embedded in practice and supported in the ways I have described, *both the individual and the school grow.* The potential of this win-win approach to individual and organizational development has drawn the attention of writers in other fields. Douglas Ready and Jay Conger (2003), in their review of leadership development in business, concluded that "executives learn leadership much more effectively from experiences than from educational courses" and that the leadership they learned that way has immediate benefits to their companies (p. 87). They called for companies themselves to "take leadership development seriously and treat it as a core business process" (p. 88).

The education world needs to pay attention to this win-win principle. The growing complexity of school administrative positions, the stress that now seems a permanent marker of most such positions, and the shrinking pools of administrative applicants make Ready and Conger's recommendations an urgent matter for many school districts. It should also awaken state departments of education and universities to their responsibilities. The vast potential of teacher leadership, meanwhile, continues to go untapped in many districts.

The learning experiences recounted in this book leave me with four recommendations to those who will, I hope, join in the effort to make performance learning truly a core function in every district. First, we must cast our net widely and encourage the leadership of many people in diverse roles in our schools. Leadership is not solely the domain of administrators. Second, we must cultivate the "I and I" dimensions of learning for these leaders. They are vital partners to the "C"; our best school leaders blend well their capacities in all three domains. Third, richer soil for the cultivation of leader knowledge will require school districts and professional development organizations, including universities, to behave differently. Most important, it will require them to make leaders' practice the fertile classroom that it clearly has been for my colleagues in Maine. And finally, aspiring and practicing leaders themselves must listen to themselves as learners and insist that their colleagues, districts, and "educational providers" do likewise. The time for treating educational leaders as passive learners must end; it is an act of leadership itself to insist that one's own learning must make a difference in one's performance.

CAST THE LEADERSHIP NET WIDE

When people talk of leadership preparation, they often allude to "farm leagues" or a "pipeline," as if there were a hierarchy of levels a person moved through to "get to be a leader." This observation is not only untrue, it is also harmful to schools. As long as we persist in this mindset, we will not only exclude talented leaders from considering formal leadership roles but also discourage those many teachers and other staff who already serve as vital leaders in our schools.

The work and culture of adults influence in complex ways educational practice and student learning. Teachers and administrators live at the center of this world and *together* shape the flow of leadership, determining its ultimate impacts on students. In Jim Spillane's (2006) terms, leadership in schools is "distributed"; it succeeds through the participation and relationships of many people and results from the "leader-plus," not the leader flying solo. The culture and social architecture of schools limit administrative authority and influence; teacher leaders, by contrast, often have relational influence that can promote innovation and strong professional norms (Donaldson, 2006). If we are to create a vibrant leadership milieu in schools, we need to cultivate leadership wherever we find willing leaders!

This means casting the net widely and keeping the doors to leadership development opportunities open to many. Schools are naturally moving in this direction as new roles for teacher leadership emerge. Professional development and school improvement opportunities now incorporate more skills and competencies in the interpersonal domain than they once did. Universities that have reformed programs in educational administration into programs in educational leadership presumably prepare leaders for a number of roles, not simply administrative ones. As we learn more about how leaders learn, our curricula and methods of teaching must expand to suit the learning needs of all types of leaders.

Our experience has taught us two things vital to casting the net widely. One is the importance of what I call "the will to lead." It's perhaps the most influential of all preconditions for leader learning. It taps into our vision, commitment, desire to make a difference on a scale broader than our own classrooms or particular jobs. The will to lead emanates from our intrapersonal domain, informed as it is by our values and philosophy, our deeper purposes for becoming educators in the first place. So when we cast our nets to find people eager to learn leadership, we need to listen to those staff members who say, I do. I want to make a bigger difference for us all.

Second, watch and listen to faculty and staff members and ask, Who makes a difference in their effectiveness here? In effect, look for members of the school community *who are already playing a leadership role*. These are teachers, coaches, counselors, and secretaries who see it as their responsibility to make the whole school better. Their interpersonal skills and knowledge have helped create strong working relationships where it counts. And here's the point: Do not treat these folks as if they know little about leadership! Use the ongoing experience they have gained as people who make a difference as the springboard for their deeper learning in the ways that this book has illustrated. Leadership—real and potential—is all around us, waiting to be cultivated.

Casting the net widely is not just about recruiting, it's about seeing the talent and will to lead that most schools have in ample quantities. And it's about ensuring that the portals to learning are expansive enough to honor the interpersonal and intrapersonal realities that surround each individual leader's work. Because that's where the most lasting learning needs to start.

HONOR THE I AND I

Leadership is a *performance* phenomenon. It cannot exist without relationships that permit communication and deliberation to happen, which, eventually, mobilizes people to action. I find it essential to remind myself of this and to ward off the assumption that leadership can be learned in the inert form it takes in books, prepackaged workshops, and other solely cognitive representations. As Ready and Conger (2003) note, it's easy to believe that learning leadership is about "the products themselves rather than the problems that need to be solved" (p. 85). If learning is to make a difference in the quality of schools, it must make a difference in leaders' performance competencies, not just in their cognitive understanding.

The I-C-I knowledge model captures the dynamism and contextual nature of performance by recognizing the key roles of the intrapersonal and the interpersonal. Our leader colleagues in Maine have illustrated throughout this book how the most powerful knowledge *emerges in action* and how these lessons are powerful *because they are applicable in action— that is, in performance.* Many of the most lasting lessons, in fact, couldn't have risen to consciousness without our leaders' continuous engagement in their efforts to lead.

Learning to lead, then, is more like learning to ride a bicycle than it is learning Darling-Hammond's (1997) helpful framework for school improvement, the state law book, or Hallinger and Murphy's (1992) correlates of instructional leadership. Yes, we can study these apt descriptions of "how it should be done," just as a 7-year-old might learn that she or he needs to hold the handlebars, sit on the seat, pedal, and steer. But the *performance* of leadership involves so much more, just as actually trying to ride a bike involves so much more. Balancing. Calming fears of crashing. Making sense of one parent's encouraging "You can do it" and another holler "Watch out for the curb!" Summoning up the courage to finally push off.

Participants in our programs do a great deal of "getting ready to lead"— the planning to perform, putting knowledge accumulated over months of reading and discussing finally into action, and the anticipation of what's going to happen once you "push off." As with bike riding, you never really know what's going to happen until it does. You never come to know if you can ride a bike until you've wobbled 15 feet more or less in the direction you'd hoped to move. As we have seen in this book, learning leaders don't gain confidence that they can lead until they've tried and learned from those around them that their performance is making a difference.

Leader learning, though, is distinctly different from learning to ride a bike. Eager 7-year-olds must eventually integrate the several moving parts of their performance task—balance, steering, pedaling, emotion—into a moving system that makes them and their bike one. Leaders face the same task, but with one huge difference: the moving parts they're trying to integrate are already moving on their own and often with a will of their own. The members of the school faculty, the superintendent, the angry parent, and the upset teacher are not evenly spaced gears on a sprocket driving the wheels! Leading them or leading with them requires abundant insight into what people want, mean, think, and feel.

As we have seen in this book, learning to lead involves immense exploration into how to carry yourself interpersonally so that these other people, hopefully willingly, function as a single moving system that helps kids learn. New learners in this process often hope to find a formula or model that works in all situations. They're thinking of themselves as the chain on the bicycle: If I can learn how to drive these gears and just keep driving, this bike will move! They learn that some fundamental principles do help them lead, but these are primarily relational in nature, not technical or mechanical. And mostly what they learn is that they've got to be adept at reading interpersonal, organizational, and intrapersonal cues, because their colleagues are not sprockets on a gear and neither are they.

Emotions are ever present in leadership performance. When they're in sync and positive, they function as a wonderful lubricant to the process of mobilization. When they're not, they are sand and gravel crunching in the gears. Learning leaders have been on the "other side"—as teachers, counselors, staff—in the relationships that create organizational emotion, and they are often painfully aware of the interpersonal missteps that throw sand and gravel into the workings of a school. But here again, the only way to understand how your own interpersonal style, your own communication skills, your own emotional signals will affect others is to push off and try.

A lasting lesson of our experience in Maine is that those who seem to have gained the most from our learning opportunities are those who can read interpersonal signals in action, can understand intrapersonally what these suggest about their own immediate performance, and then can adjust that performance interpersonally and cognitively within minutes or even seconds. They have learned through direct and indirect feedback how they tend to function in various situations. Their growing self-awareness in leadership action informs their growing ability to self-manage or to adjust performance in the middle of the action, if necessary.

This can be difficult and risky work. To read the signals from your environment, you need to see and hear clearly, to be honest about how the part you are playing is shaping events, and to be willing to tackle the "pebbles in your shoe." Not everyone feels safe enough to do this. For some, the will to lead isn't strong enough to make the risks worth it. And for others the sheer complexity of blending the interpersonal and intrapersonal with the often more clearly articulated cognitive can be overwhelming.

Eventually we learn to ride bicycles through repeated efforts and inevitable scrapes and bumps, fighting through fear and discouragement to the elation of actually maintaining balance, speed, and direction enough to feel the wind blow through our hair and to hear the cheers of our personal fans. It takes time. It takes perseverance and lots of practice. It helps to have fans. The same goes for learning to lead.

CONSCIOUSLY CULTIVATE LEADERSHIP

The most basic condition to support leader learning is a professional culture that encourages and even insists that every leader continually ask,

How do I know that my efforts are helping students learn? The schools and school districts where this culture thrives are places where principals, teacher leaders, and central office leaders seek, find, and use the feedback that helps them know how they're performing. They are places where the risks of setting learning goals and of trying out new ways of behaving are rewarded. They are places where the "top leaders" of the district consciously cultivate opportunities for those willing to lead to find solid answers to this "how do I know" question.

Professional cultures don't just happen. A culture that consciously cultivates leadership values performance over prose or posture. It is not enough, as Peter Senge (1990) puts it, for our leaders to "become speech makers rather than leaders . . . [to] become 'true believers' rather than learners" (p. 357). To truly help their schools grow, leaders cannot merely talk a new talk while continuing to behave in the same old ways. Their growth—and that of their schools—comes from the creative tension between the ideal and the real, from the "pebbles in their shoes" that chafe when their own performance doesn't match what the school needs to grow.

The top leaders in our school districts and schools—those formal leaders to whom others look—can take a page from effective businesses in this regard. Indeed, some, such as John Wiens (2006) and Rebecca Van der Bogert (2006), have. They place high on their priorities in word and deed the cultivation of leadership within their districts rather than assuming that they can hire it or buy it. As Corazon Aquino has put it, "We cannot, of course, just place an order for such men and women to be or to lead. . . . Such people are not made to order. They make themselves that way" (in Senge, 1990, p. 359).

What is essential in this learning culture, beyond this overarching emphasis on learning for every person? *Opportunities and methods for professional learning need to be embedded in work routines.* They need to become part of "how we do things around here." Principals, teacher leaders, and central office leaders need to create opportunities to reflect—to follow leadership activities with a time to examine "how it went" with help from steady and insightful colleagues. They need to make the Reflective Learning process and the Performance Learning Cycle part of the vernacular. They need to find and use a structure for goal-setting and learning that works for them along the lines of our Leadership Development Plans. They need to remind one another to attend to all three dimensions of learning, the I, the C, and the I. And they need to observe one another, coach one another, and support one another.

Small *colleague-critic teams* have proved an excellent way to structure activities that embed this culture of learning for leaders. A number of schools in Maine and at least one large district have made these clusters of 3–5 a permanent resource, scheduling time for them to meet in the day, during faculty meetings, after school, and during professional development days. We've found protocols immensely helpful for such teams as a way to structure reflection on practice so that every person has a turn and participates. Many of the lessons we've learned about these teams are now part of the current professional learning community movement (DuFour, Eaker, & DuFour, 2006; Norris et al., 2002).

It's essential, as well, that professional development opportunities outside the district, including graduate programs in educational leadership and administration, *blend with these internal structures and culture*. Professional developers and professors can help to create them by making leaders' practice their "classrooms" and leaders' performance their central focus. All learning is embedded in schools and performance, not postponed until an internship or relegated to isolated case studies. One certain way to make this happen is to include in all learning frameworks the interpersonal and intrapersonal domains. As the Landscape in Chapter 9 illustrates, when a professor or workshop leader honors these immediate realities in the leader's work, she or he has committed her- or himself to forms of teaching that professionals find relevant, meaningful, and tied to their own practice.

Approached in this manner, professional development and graduate study frame curriculum and learning methods that stimulate learning not just *for* the work "back at school" but *in* the work at school. They focus on cultivating skills and competencies that learners need rather than on "product-focused quick-fixes" and "make-believe metrics that measure [learning] activity rather than capability" (Ready & Conger, 2003, p. 88). They provide cognitive frameworks, but they also offer ways for learners to find themselves and their schools in those frameworks and to integrate them into their own learning plans—and particularly into the interpersonal and intrapersonal domains. Learning opportunities of this kind will make it safe to try out new performance strategies, to gather feedback and reflect on it, and to fold new ways of thihking and behaving into one's repertoire through "lots of practice and repetition" (Goleman, Boyatzis, & McKee, 2002, p. 103).

Senge and others (Boyatzis, Cowen, & Kolb, 1995; Drago-Severson, 2004; Mezirow, 2000) remind us that the learner is the primary mover in this process. As Senge notes:

> "Really deep learning is a process that inevitably is driven by the learner, not by someone else. And it always involves moving back and forth between a domain of thinking and a domain of action. . . . Learning always takes place

in a context where you are taking action. So we need to find ways to get [educators] really working together; we need to create an environment where they can continually reflect on what they are doing and learn more and more." (in O'Neil, 1995; p. 20)

Many of our participants and the educators around them see the potential of this approach to truly make a difference in their schools. It resonates with their natural ways of learning. It legitimizes their practice and their "pebbles." And, as Goleman and colleagues (2002) put it, it offers a way out of "recycling their problems [by repeating old behaviors based on old attitudes and habits]. . . . In the rush to achieve their goals and complete their tasks, [leaders] short themselves on learning to lead better. Often a leader will try a new approach once or twice, and then apply it—without giving himself the chance to *practice* it" (p. 157; emphasis in the original).

The I-C-I model of learning helps leaders understand how their hands and hearts—the interpersonal and intrapersonal domains—are integral to their heads, and why interpersonal skills and intrapersonal sensibilities *take time and practice* to develop. The model offers districts, professional developers, and professors a language for creating a more continuous and more productive learning environment for all leaders.

CHAMPION LEARNING—INCLUDING YOUR OWN

The more deeply resonant kind of performance learning that we engender in our programs depends on learners' finding their own learning paths. To literally "encourage" educators in this way calls for an environment that feels safe and promotes authenticity. The elaborate curriculum we generated seeks to promote such a culture. For most participants, it worked: we've seen busy educators from diverse schools and roles gradually drop their old habits of mind and of learning and open themselves up to seeing the interpersonal, cognitive, and intrapersonal realities of leadership in their own cases. To look more closely at their own styles, knowledge bases, and relationships at work and at themselves took courage and the confidence to be vulnerable and to trust. For most, it was intense but immensely rewarding learning.

Becoming open to learning as a leader is tough because we often think that leadership is inborn rather than learned. We get into it because we hope to discover if we "have the right stuff." Much of that right stuff, though, is hard to pin down, because most leadership knowledge is implicit or tacit. Goleman and colleagues (2002) describe it this way:

> Virtually none of these lessons [about how to lead] involves explicit instruc-
> tion in elements of leadership—they arise naturally in the course of life. . . .
> Each time an individual heads a team, for instance, he'll most readily repeat
> what he did before as a team leader. . . . All this learning goes on tacitly,
> most of the time without people even being aware that they are mastering
> such lessons, in what amounts to stealth learning. (p. 155)

What we've learned is that bringing some of this stealth learning out into
the sunlight by making it "talkable" can go a long way toward opening
educators to their own developmental challenges as leaders. Most important, it can help them evaluate whether their existing leadership knowledge is working for their schools and to gain some level of control over
how to improve.

We find that expressly creating group conditions that support learning simply asserts for all the importance of "talking about your and my
learning." It can be tough to do this in a gathering of ambitious educators.
They typically want to solve problems, talk about solutions to teaching
challenges, or share best practices from their schools. And these, of course,
are rich nutrients for the learning process. The power of the superintendent here is immense; her or his example as a learner and initiative as a
culture builder has been critical to the success of leadership development—
and thus of leadership itself (Van der Bogert, 2006; Wiens, 2006).

Making learning talkable isn't the same as telling others what works
for me at my school. That's more like teaching than learning. Learning
communities begin at a different place: they come together to share performance challenges with one another—the pebbles they feel in their shoes
as they seek to walk the leadership road. They are rich with encouragement to probe more deeply into those experiences, to bring assumptions
and unspoken judgments about other people into the open, and to help
learners know what they can shape in the leadership situation and what
they cannot. They are marked by the amount and intensity of *listening*
rather than the amount and intensity of *telling*.

Championing leader learning, then, means finding ways that every
leader can voice her or his aspirations and doubts. It means asserting the
important goal of finding a leadership role that fits and thus where each
leader can thrive and help a school thrive. Stealth learning, in this regard,
is really self-authored learning; it means making a central place for the
leader's own personal conditions, capabilities, learning styles, and dreams
in the search for the best way she or he can make a school sing.

The I-C-I framework helps. It asserts that leading is complex because
it's not simply a matter of learning cognitive strategies and techniques and
going forth to implement them. Effective implementation of effective prac-

tices hinges a great deal on interpersonal knowledge and skills—and these are applied in an ever changing interpersonal staff and faculty environment. In other words, leaders need to be vigilant about this environment and ready to learn about the people around them and what's necessary for their mobilization.

But most fundamentally, the I-C-I model legitimizes the learning leader's feelings, doubts, and needs by including the intrapersonal. That is perhaps why many participants in our programs come to treasure most their learning in this dimension. It gives them a way to be honest with themselves. It helps them to learn to be reflective about their own performance and to understand that they bring both assets and liabilities to their work as leaders. So it has allowed them to say, It's OK that I can't spring full blown as an effective leader in my school. It's like anything else in life, I need to work on becoming one.

The road to championing our own learning starts by recognizing that we're in this to discover how leading works "for me" and "in my school," not merely to learn what others have written about leadership and how it works. This can be difficult. It's messy because it involves people; relationships; feelings; and deeply held beliefs, habits, and practices. It requires admitting that "I don't have the answers" but also that "I'm committed to working with you to find solutions." Central office, school boards, and members of the public often want sure-footed, solution-toting administrators, so learning leaders often must advocate, just as sure-footedly, for the time and room for learning. As Roland Barth puts it, "Once you declare yourself learn*ed,* your chances of successfully leading a learning institution like a school have ended" (personal correspondence).

Taking the personal route to learning and making effective performance the measure of success, as the leaders in this book have, takes courage. After all, they are stretching themselves beyond their comfort levels and, in the process, stretching their colleagues, their students, and sometimes their communities beyond theirs as well. A letter I wrote in May 2003 to members of a cohort completing their 2-year stint in the Maine School Leadership Network captured well my sentiments in this regard:

> Dear Colleague:
> You have taught me an important lesson (a lesson I need to be retaught periodically) about school leadership: It's not always welcomed by everyone at school, and especially by those who might benefit from it most! We all assume we need administrators because they've almost always been there. But leaders? Now, that's something different! Someone who believes that a school can make a difference, not just that individual teachers, counselors, or

coaches make a difference. Someone who allows herself or himself to be carried along on the power of this belief, beyond wondering if it's going to look pushy to others or if it's going to threaten the "powers that be." Someone who has the skills to share that belief, to welcome others into it, to honor others with equally heartfelt beliefs—as long as kids are at the center of it. These are who you are, you leaders!

I'm reminded, too, of what this journey has required of you. The time, the reading, the journal-writing, the portfolios, the drives down [winding, rural] Route 11, the CCT meetings in the cold, dark afternoons, the e-mails and phone calls from Linda [their MSLN facilitator]. . . . But most of all MSLN required that you make a choice: the choice of stepping out of your old niche as a teacher, counselor, administrator, or ed tech and to mold yourself a new niche where you could actively shape your school for the better. This choice to "make yourself a leader" (sounds brash!) is, in large part, what leadership is about. What it takes, more than anything, is a commitment to doing it and to casting a critical eye on yourself as you do it.

As a cohort, you've been a very special group . . . a pretty diverse group who nonetheless has thought together, challenged one another, and shared personal and professional doubts and successes. I attribute the rich learning environment you have cultivated in part to Linda's patient and insightful facilitation; but it's also something that each one of you has shaped in important ways (with humor, with poetry, with honesty, with warmth, and always with a dedication to pushing your own understanding of yourself and of others further along). You haven't just "partici- pated" in MSLN, you have each lived a commitment to your own growth and to your school's improvement through MSLN.

As I think of the place of MSLN on the education landscape of Maine, I like to think that, in its small and very personal way, the network is helping educators more deeply understand how impor- tant their own learning is to the improvement of their schools. As each one of you has made it plain to your school colleagues that you *are* learning and *using* that learning to shape the school, you encour- age others to do likewise. You give them hope, you bring them together to support each other, and you raise the bar for everyone. And in this fashion, the network spreads a belief that schools can be better and, with many people learning in them (big and small), there will be many leaders helping to move each school along to where *all* kids are learning in richer and more profound ways.

Thank you so much for joining MSLN and for helping to lead it as you have. We have all been so fortunate for the skills, wisdom, support, and undying faith that Linda has brought to this experience. So, too, have we been fortunate for the ways that each of you has made it as wonderful an experience as it has been.
Please stay in touch,
Gordon

Leaders who discover themselves as learners often become passionate advocates for a new conception of leadership centered around adults' learning. Instead of viewing schooling as a technical endeavor with one-size-fits-all "best practices" that leaders mandate, they present a case for schooling as a responsive invention of practices, a search for the best learning for each child. Successful teaching draws from a rich repertoire of methods and resources to stimulate learning in every child, every day. Learning curves stay steep for adults so they can keep them steep for kids. Schools are creative, generative, and responsive. Their leaders' work is to cultivate learning at every turn, starting with their own.

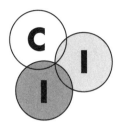

A Framework for Assessing Leadership Learning

WE DEVELOPED the following taxonomy of leader knowledge to assist leaders and us to assess learning needs, set learning goals, and collect performance feedback on progress.

COGNITIVE

KNOWLEDGE ABOUT TEACHING AND LEARNING

An effective school leader has expertise in learning and teaching, assessment of learning, and instructional design and delivery for children and adults.

Understands intellectual, social, psychological, and moral development throughout the lifespan.

KNOWLEDGE ABOUT SCHOOL IMPROVEMENT

An effective school leader understands how schools improve their performance and how leaders facilitate organizational learning and growth.

Diagnoses organizational characteristics and needs, using organizational theories and research as appropriate.

157

Understands teaching/developmental strategies to enhance students' cognitive, social, psychological, and moral development.

Understands procedures for assessment of student needs and for instructional planning and evaluation to address them.

Understands professional learning and intervention strategies to enhance staff expertise in above strategies and procedures.

Corresponding to:
ISLLC Principles I, II, III, V
NCATE Proficiencies #7, 8, 9, 11, 15

Understands systems of organizational planning and evaluation necessary to establish continual improvement for the school/district.

Understands models and theories of leadership related to organizational effectiveness and improvement in schools.

Understands how social, cultural, economic, and political forces shape student needs, school goals, and staff performance.

ISLLC Principles I, II, III, V, VI
NCATE Proficiencies #7, 9, 11, 14, 15, 18

INTERPERSONAL

CAPACITY TO CULTIVATE WORKING RELATIONSHIPS

An effective school leader cultivates effective working relationships with and among staff, students, parents, and community.

Understands relational dynamics: how relationships form and are sustained for effective individual and collective performance.

Understands leaders' roles in forming and sustaining productive working relationships in school and community environments.

Accurately judges how others feel, what others think, and what others need in order to feel valued and productive in working relationships.

CAPACITY TO MOBILIZE OTHERS TO ACTION

An effective school leader mobilizes others to improve practices and performance so that the school's success with every child improves.

Diagnoses the capacity of groups for action and facilitates the group's goal setting, action planning, and follow-through.

Diagnoses the performance capacity of individuals and facilitates engagement in and sustenance of improved individual performance.

Balances improvement goals and plans with groups' and individuals' capacities to learn and to sustain efforts to improve performance.

Facilitates trusting, respectful relationships among individuals with differing views, talents, backgrounds and dispositions.

Monitors her/his own participation in working relationships and adjusts her/his performance to strengthen relationships.

Corresponding to:
ISLLC Principles I, II, III, IV, V
NCATE Proficiencies #9, 10, 11, 13

Understands how organizational factors shape groups' and individuals' capacities to act and intervenes productively to influence organizational and political dynamics and decisions.

ISLLC Principles I, II, IV
NCATE Proficiencies #9, 10, 13, 14

INTRAPERSONAL

FOUNDATION OF LEADERSHIP BELIEFS

CAPACITY FOR SELF-AWARENESS AND SELF-MANAGEMENT

ASSESSMENT OF LEADER CAPACITIES AND CHOICES

An effective school leader articulates a coherent and defensible leadership philosophy that supports high student and school performance.

An effective school leader accurately assesses her/his performance style and effectiveness (self-awareness) and adjusts her/his performance to enhance effectiveness (self-management).

An effective school leader accurately understands her/his assets and liabilities as a leader and chooses roles that are productive and sustainable for both the school and herself/himself.

Articulates her/his core values and evidence to support them regarding effective learning and teaching, school programs and structures, the roles of collaboration, power, and authority in leadership.

Employs in-action reflective and analytic skills to adjust leadership practices (behaviors, thoughts, feelings) during performance (in-action reflection).

Uses appropriate leadership models and evidence from performance to assess assets and liabilities.

Draws upon this platform in a transparent manner in forming working relationships and facilitating action-strategies to improve student learning (*a plan to lead*).

Draws upon this platform in her/his *plan to reflect*—to evaluate the school's progress and her/his own effectiveness as a leader.

Analyzes leadership events and her/his part in them to assess the effectiveness of her/his behaviors, ideas, and style in those events (the *plan to reflect*).

Identifies how her/his own specific skills, knowledge levels, and dispositions shape how she/he performs in specific situations. Creates *plans to learn* that address performance needs that are identified.

Integrates cognitive, interpersonal, and intrapersonal knowledge to frame a *plan to lead* appropriate to student learning needs, staff and community capacities, and her/his own capacities to lead.

Assesses the overall productivity and sustainability of leadership roles and relationships for the school and herself/himself.

Uses this assessment information to make choices regarding leadership roles and career paths.

Uses this holistic assessment to shape her/his role, engage colleagues' leader talents to complement hers/his, and advocate for ongoing learning and support.

Corresponding to:
ISLLC Principles I–VI
NCATE Proficiencies
#2, 8, 9, 10, 11, 12, 14, 15, 18

ISLLC Principles I–VI
NCATE Proficiencies
#2, 11, 12, 14

ISLLC Principles I–VI
NCATE Proficiencies
#11, 14

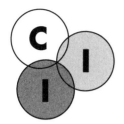 References

Ackerman, R., & Mackenzie, S. (2007). *Uncovering teacher leadership: Essays and voices from the field.* Thousand Oaks, CA: Corwin.

Ackerman, R., & Maslin-Ostrowski, P. (2002). *The wounded leader: How real leadership emerges in times of crisis.* San Francisco: Jossey-Bass.

Argyris, C. (1991, April). Teaching smart people to learn. *Harvard Business Review, 69*(3), 99–109.

Argyris, C. (1993). *Knowledge for action.* San Francisco: Jossey-Bass.

Argyris, C. (1999). Tacit knowledge in management. In R. Sternberg & J. Horvath (Eds.), *Tacit knowledge in professional practice: Researcher and practitioner perspectives* (pp. 123–140). Mahwah, NJ: Erlbaum Associates.

Argyris, C., & Schön, D. A. (1974). *Theory in practice: Increasing professional effectiveness.* San Francisco: Jossey-Bass.

Barth, R. (1990). *Improving schools from within.* San Francisco: Jossey-Bass.

Barth, R. (1997). *The principal learner: A work in progress.* Cambridge, MA: International Network of Principals' Centers, Harvard University.

Barth, R. (2001). *Learning by heart.* San Francisco: Jossey-Bass.

Black, W., & Murtadha, K. (2006). Toward a signature pedagogy in educational leadership preparation and program assessment. Bloomington: University Council for Educational Administration, Indiana University.

Blasé, J., & Anderson, G. (1995). *The micropolitics of leadership in education: From control to empowerment.* New York: Teachers College Press.

Bolman, L., & Deal, T. (2005). *Reframing organizations* (3rd ed.). San Francisco: Jossey-Bass.

Boyatzis, R., Cowen, R., & Kolb, D. (1995). *Innovations in professional education: Steps on a journey from teaching to learning.* San Francisco: Jossey-Bass.

Boyatzis, R., Stubbs, E., & Taylor, S. (2002). Learning cognitive and emotional intelligence competencies through graduate management education. *Academy of Management Learning and Education, 1*(2), 150–162.

Bredeson, P. (1995). Building a professional knowledge base in educational administration: Opportunities and obstacles. In R. Donmoyer, M. Imber, & J. Scheurich (Eds.), *The knowledge base in educational administration* (pp. 47–73). Albany: SUNY Press.

Bridges, E., & Hallinger, P. (1997). *Using problem-based learning to prepare educational leaders.* Mahwah, NJ: Lawrence Erlbaum Associates.

Brookfield, S. (1995). *Becoming a critically reflective teacher.* San Francisco: Jossey-Bass.

Brown, J., & Duguid, P. (1991, April). Organizational learning and communities-of-practice: Toward a unified theory of working, learning, and innovation. *Organization Science, 2*(1), 40–57.

Buchanan, C. (1996). *Choosing to lead: Women and the crisis of American values.* Boston: Beacon Press.

Buck, R. (1993). Spontaneous communication and the foundation of the interpersonal self. In U. Neisser (Ed.), *The perceived self: Ecological and interpersonal sources of self-knowledge* (pp. 216–236). Cambridge: Cambridge University Press.

Bryk, A., & Schneider, B. (2002). *Trust in schools: A core resource for improvement.* New York: Russell Sage Foundation.

Cotton, K. (2000). *The schooling practices that matter most.* Seattle, WA: Northwest Regional Educational Laboratory.

Covey, S. (1989). *The seven habits of highly effective people.* New York: Free Press.

Covey, S. (1991). *Principle-centered leadership.* New York: Summit Books.

Crowe, S. (1999). *Since strangling isn't an option: Dealing with difficult people: Common problems, and uncommon solutions.* Berkeley, CA: Perigee.

Danielson, C. (1996). *Enhancing professional practice: A framework for teaching.* Alexandria, VA: Association for Supervision and Curriculum Development.

Daresh, J. (2001). *Leaders helping leaders.* Thousand Oaks, CA: Corwin.

Darling-Hammond, L. (1997). *The right to learn: A blueprint for creating schools that work.* San Francisco: Jossey-Bass.

Donaldson, G. A., Jr. (1998). Sharing the challenges: Critic-colleague teams and leadership development. In R. van der Bogert (Ed.), *Making learning communities work; The critical role of leader as learner* (pp. 21–28). San Francisco: Jossey-Bass.

Donaldson, G. A., Jr. (2006). *Cultivating leadership in schools: Connecting people, purpose, and practice.* New York: Teachers College Press.

Donaldson, G. A., Jr., Bowe, L. M., Mackenzie, S. V., & Marnik, G. F. (2004). Learning from leadership work: Maine pioneers a school leadership network. *Phi Delta Kappan, 85*(7), 539–545.

Donaldson, G., & Marnik, G. (1995). *Becoming better leaders.* Thousand Oaks, CA: Corwin.

Donaldson, G. A., Jr., & Sanderson, D. (1996). *Working together in schools: A guide for educators.* Thousand Oaks, CA: Corwin.

Drago-Severson, E. (2004). *Helping teachers learn: Principal leadership for adult growth and development.* Thousand Oaks, CA: Corwin.

DuFour, R., Eaker, R., & DuFour, R. (Eds.). (2005). *On common ground: The power of professional learning communities.* Bloomington, IN: National Educational Service.

Ellison, J., & Hayes, C. (2005). *Effective school leadership: Developing principals through cognitive coaching.* Norwood, MA: Christopher-Gordon.

Evans, R. (1996). *The human side of school change: Reform, resistance, and the real-life problems of innovation.* San Francisco: Jossey-Bass.

Fullan, M. (2003). *Leadership and sustainability: System thinkers in action.* Thousand Oaks, CA: Corwin.

Gardner, H. (1983). *Frames of mind: The theory of multiple intelligences.* New York: Basic Books.

Garmston, R., & Wellman, B. (1999). *The adaptive school: A sourcebook for developing collaborative groups.* Norwood, MA: Christopher-Gordon.

Glaude, C. (2005). *Protocols for professional learning conversations: Cultivating the art and discipline.* Courtney, Canada: Connections.

Goleman, D. (1995). *Emotional intelligence.* New York: Bantam Books.

Goleman, D. (1998a, November/December). What makes a leader? *Harvard Business Review, 76*(2), 93–102.

Goleman, D. (1998b). *Working with emotional intelligence.* New York: Bantam Books.

Goleman, D. (2006). *Social intelligence: The new science of human relationships.* New York: Bantam Dell.

Goleman, D., Boyatzis, R., & McKee, A. (2002). *Primal leadership: Realizing the power of emotional intelligence.* Cambridge, MA: Harvard Business School Press.

Hall, J., & Bernieri, F. (2001). *Interpersonal sensitivity: Theory and measurement.* Mahwah, NJ: Lawrence Erlbaum Associates.

Hallinger, P., & Murphy, J. (1992). The principalship in an era of transformation. *Journal of Educational Administration, 30*(3), 19–28.

Hargreaves, A., & Fink, D. (2006). *Sustainable leadership.* San Francisco: Jossey-Bass.

Heifetz, R. (1994). *Leadership without easy answers.* Cambridge, MA: Belknap Press/ Harvard University Press.

Heifetz, R., & Linsky, M. (2004, April). When leadership spells danger: Leading meaningful change in education takes courage, commitment, and political savvy. *Educational Leadership, 62*(8), 33–37.

Helgesen, S. (1995). *The female advantage: Women's ways of leading.* New York: Currency-Doubleday.

Hopkins, R. (1994, April). "Like life itself": Narrative and the revitalization of educational practice. Paper presented at the annual meeting of the John Dewey Society, New Orleans.

Interstate School Licensure Consortium (1996). *Standards for school leaders.* Washington, DC: Council of Chief State School Officers.

Isenhart, M., & Spangle, M. (2000). *Collaborative approaches to resolving conflict.* Thousand Oaks, CA: Sage.

Johnson, D., & Johnson, F. (1995). *Joining together: Group theory and group skills* (5th ed.). Boston: Allyn & Bacon.

Katzenmayer, M., & Moller, G. (2001). *Awakening the sleeping giant* (2nd ed.). Thousand Oaks, CA: Corwin.

Kegan, R., & Lahey, L. (2001). *How the way we talk can change the way we work: Seven Languages for Transformation.* San Francisco: Jossey-Bass.

Kidder, R. (2004). *Moral courage: Taking action when your values are put to the test.* New York: William Morrow.

Kolb, D. (1984). *Experiential learning: Experience as the source of learning and development.* Upper Saddle River, NJ: Prentice-Hall.

Kolb, D. (1999). Learning Style Inventory—version 3: Technical specifications. TRG Hay/McBer, Training Resources Group. 116 Huntington Ave., Boston MA 02116, trg_mcber@haygroup.com.

Kolb, D., Boyatzis, R., & Mainemelis, C. (2000). Experiential learning theory: Previous research and new directions. In R. Sternberg & L. Zhang (Eds.), *Perspectives in cognitive, learning, and thinking styles.* Mahwah, NJ: Lawrence Erlbaum.

Korthagen, F., & Vasalos, A. (2005). Levels in reflection: Core reflection as a means to enhance professional growth. *Teachers and Teaching: Theory and Practice 11*(1), 47–71.

Kouzes, J., & Posner, B. (2007). *The leadership challenge (The Leadership Profile Inventory).* San Francisco: Jossey-Bass.

Lambert, K., Walker, D., Zimmerman, D., Cooper, J., Lambert, M. D., Gardner, M., & Slack, P. J. (1995). *The constructivist leader.* New York: Teachers College Press.

Lave, J., & Wenger, E. (1991). *Situated learning: Legitimate peripheral participation.* Cambridge: Cambridge University Press.

Leithwood, K., Louis, K. S., Anderson, S., & Wahlstrom, K. (2004). *How leadership influences student learning. Learning from the Leadership Project.* Atlanta, GA: The Wallace Foundation.

Levin, H. (2006, November). Can research improve educational leadership? *Educational Researcher, 35*(8), 38–43.

Lewis, T., Amini, F., & Lannon, R. (2000). *A general theory of love.* New York: Vintage.

Lieberman, A., & Miller, L. (2001). *Teachers caught in the action: Professional development that matters.* New York: Teachers College Press.

Mackenzie, S., & Marnik, G. (2006). *Coaching school leaders: New role for university professors.* Unpublished paper. Orono, ME: University of Maine College of Education and Human Development.

Maine Department of Education. (1998). *Promising futures: An invitation to improve our secondary schools.* Augusta, ME: Author.

Marnik, G. (1997). *The professional development of school leaders: Exploring the thought and practice of learning about leadership.* Unpublished doctoral dissertation, University of Maine, Orono.

McDonald, J. (1996). *Redesigning school: Lessons for the 21st century.* San Francisco: Jossey-Bass.

Meier, D. (2002). *In schools we trust: Creating communities of learning in an era of testing and standardization.* Boston: Beacon.

Mezirow, J. (2000). Learning to think like an adult: Core concepts of transformation theory. In J. Mezirow & Associates (Eds.), *Learning as transformation: Critical perspectives on a theory in progress* (pp. 3–33). San Francisco: Jossey-Bass.

Murphy, J. (1992). *The landscape of leadership preparation: Reframing the education of school administrators.* Thousand Oaks, CA: Corwin.

Myers-Briggs Foundation. (2006). The Myers-Briggs Type Indicator.myers-briggs.org

National School Reform Faculty. (2005). *Protocols.* Bloomington, IN: Harmony Education Center. www.nsrfharmony.org/resources.html

Neisser, U. (1993). *The perceived self: Ecological and interpersonal sources of self-knowledge.* Cambridge: Cambridge University Press.

Norris, C., Barnett, B., Basom, M., & Yerkes, D. (2002). *Developing educational leaders: A working model; The learning community in action.* New York: Teachers College Press.

O'Neil, J. (1995, April). On schools as learning organizations: A conversation with Peter Senge. *Educational Leadership, 63*(8), 20–23.

Osterman, K. (1998). Using constructivism to bridge the theory/practice gap. Paper presented at the annual meeting of the American Educational Research Association, San Diego, CA.

Osterman, K., & Kottkamp, R. (1993). *Reflective practice for educators.* Thousand Oaks, CA: Corwin.

Palmer, P. (1997). *The courage to teach.* San Francisco: Jossey-Bass.

Philbrick, N. (2003). *Sea of Glory.* New York: Penguin.

Pratt, A. D., Tripp, C., & Ogden, W. (2000). *The skillful leader: Confronting mediocre teaching.* Acton, MA: Ready About Press.

Ready, D., & Conger, J. (2003, Spring). Why leadership-development efforts fail. *MIT Sloan Management Review,* pp. 83–88.

Rees, F. (1991). *How to lead work teams: Facilitation skills.* San Francisco: Jossey-Bass/Pfeifer.

Riggio, R. (2001). Interpersonal sensitivity research and organizational psychology: Theoretical and methodological applications. In J. Hall & F. Bernieri (Eds.), *Interpersonal sensitivity: Theory and measurement* (pp. 305–318). Mahwah, NJ: Lawrence Erlbaum Associates.

Schön, D. (1983). *The reflective practitioner.* New York: Basic Books.

Senge, P. (1990). *The fifth discipline: The art and practice of the learning organization.* New York: Doubleday.

Sergiovanni, T. (2005). *Strengthening the heartbeat: Leading and learning together in schools.* San Francisco: Jossey-Bass.

Spillane, J. (2006). *Distributed leadership.* San Francisco: Jossey-Bass.

Starratt, R. (2004). *Ethical leadership.* San Francisco: Jossey-Bass.

Sternberg, R. (1999). Epilogue: What do we know about tacit knowledge? Making the tacit become explicit. In R. Sternberg & J. Horvath (Eds.), *Tacit knowledge in professional practice: Researcher and practitioner perspectives* (pp. 231–236). Mahwah, NJ: Lawrence Erlbaum Associates.

Sternberg. R. (2007). Who are the bright children? The cultural context of being and acting intelligent. *Educational Researcher, 36*(3), 148–155.

Sternberg, R., Forsythe, G., Hedlund, J., Horvath, J., Wagner, R., Williams, W., Snook, S., & Grigorenko, E. (2000). *Practical intelligence in everyday life.* Cambridge: Cambridge University Press.

Sternberg, R. J., & Horvath, J. A. (Eds.). (1999). *Tacit knowledge in professional practice: Researcher and practitioner perspectives.* Mahwah, NJ: Lawrence Erlbaum Associates.

Tannen, D. (1995). *Talking from 9 to 5: Women and men in the workplace: Language, sex, and power.* New York: Avon.

Tannen, D. (1986). *That's not what I meant: How conversational style makes or breaks your relationships with others.* New York: Ballantine.

Torff, B. (1999). Tacit knowledge in teaching: Folk pedagogy and teacher education. In R. Sternberg & J. Horvath (Eds.), *Tacit knowledge in professional practice* (pp. 195–214). Mahwah, NJ: Lawrence Erlbaum Associates.

Tschannen-Moran, M. (2004). *Trust matters: Leadership for successful schools.* San Francisco: Jossey-Bass.

Ulmer, W. (1999). Military learnings: A practitioner's perspective. In R. Sternberg & J. Horvath (Eds.), *Tacit knowledge in professional practice* (pp. 59–71). Mahwah, NJ: Erlbaum Associates.

Vaill, P. (1989). *Managing as a performing art: New ideas for a world of chaotic change.* San Francisco: Jossey-Bass.

Van der Bogert, R. (2006). Democracy during hard times. In P. Kelleher & R. Van der Bogert (Eds.), *Voices for democracy: 105th yearbook of the National Society for the Study of Education* (pp. 146–169). Malden, MA: Blackwell.

Wenger, E. (1999). *Communities of practice: Learning, meaning, and identity.* Cambridge: Cambridge University Press.

Wiens, J. R. (2006). Educational leadership as civic humanism. In *Voices for democracy: 105th yearbook of the National Society for the Study of Education* (pp. 199–225). Malden, MA: Blackwell.

York-Barr, J., & Duke, K. (2004). What do we know about teacher leadership? Findings from two decades of scholarship. *Review of Educational Research, 74*(3), 255–316.

Zebrowitz, L. (2001). Groping for the elephant of interpersonal sensitivity. In J. A. Hall & F. J. Bernieri (Eds.), *Interpersonal sensitivity: Theory and measurement* (pp. 333–352). Mawah, NJ: Lawrence Erlbaum Associates.

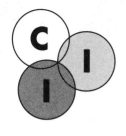

List of Resources for Cultivating Leadership Knowledge

THE COGNITIVE DOMAIN

Instructional Literacy

We encourage our colleagues to tap into the best resources available in journals and professional literature regarding student learning, assessment, instructional methods, and curriculum. Often, their professional development activities at school and other graduate course work are rich resources. We find these particularly helpful:

Allen, D., & Blythe, T. (2004). *The facilitator's book of questions: Tools for looking together at student and teacher work.* New York: Teachers College Press.

Bransford, J., Brown, A., & Cocking, R. (2003). *How people learn: Brain, mind, experience and school.* Washington, DC: National Academy Press.

Cotton, K. (2000). *The schooling practices that matter most.* Seattle, WA: Northwest Regional Educational Laboratory.

Danielson, C. (1996). *Enhancing professional practice: A framework for teaching.* Alexandria, VA: Association for Supervision and Curriculum Development.

Darling-Hammond, L. (1997). *The right to learn: A blueprint for creating schools that work.* San Francisco: Jossey-Bass.

Marzano, R. (2003). *What works in schools: Translating research into action.* Alexandria, VA: Association for Supervision and Curriculum Development.

National Board for Professional Teaching Standards. (2002). *What teachers should*

know and be able to do. Arlington, VA: National Board for Teaching Professional Standards.
Saphier, J., & Gower, R. (1997). *The skillful teacher: Building your teaching skills.* Acton, MA: Research for Better Teaching.

Organizational Literacy

In addition to many useful articles from professional journals and materials from reform centers such as the Coalition for Essential Schools, we draw on the following rich resources:

Barth, R. (1990). *Improving schools from within.* San Francisco: Jossey-Bass.
Bolman, L., & Deal, T. (2005). *Reframing organizations.* 3rd ed. San Francisco: Jossey-Bass.
Evans, R. (1996). *The human side of school change: Reform, resistance, and the real-life problems of innovation.* San Francisco: Jossey-Bass.
Fullan, M. (2001). *The new meaning of educational change.* New York: Teachers College Press.
Garmston, R., & Wellman, B. (1999). *The adaptive school: A sourcebook for developing collaborative groups.* Norwood, MA: Christopher-Gordon.
Johnson, S. M. (1990). *Teachers at work: Achieving success in our schools.* New York: Basic Books.
Lambert, L., Walker, D., Zimmerman, D., Cooper, J., Lambert, M., Gardner, M., & Slack, P. J. (1995). *The constructivist leader.* New York: Teachers College Press.
Lieberman, A., & Miller, L. (2001). *Teachers caught in the action: Professional development that matters.* New York: Teachers College Press.
Meier, D. (2002) *In schools we trust: Creating communities of learning in an era of testing and standardization.* Boston: Beacon.
Wagner, T. (1994). *How schools change: Lessons from three communities.* Boston: Beacon.

THE INTERPERSONAL DOMAIN

Books and articles that examine effective interactional patterns and skills in work settings are increasingly available, particularly in business. Although interpersonal skill and sensitivity rarely result from such cognitive sources alone, those resources that break down the processes of facilitation, intervention, conflict management, and the like have offered participants excellent protocols and diagnostic frameworks to guide their performance learning. Among the resources we've found useful are the following:

Argyris, C., & Schön, D. A. (1974). *Theory in practice: Increasing professional effectiveness.* San Francisco: Jossey-Bass.
Donaldson, G., & Sanderson, D. (1996). *Working together in schools: A guide for educators.* Thousand Oaks, CA: Corwin.

Glaude, C. (2005). *Protocols for professional learning conversations: Cultivating the art and discipline.* Courtenay, Canada: Connections.

Goleman, D. (2006). *Social intelligence: The new science of human relationships.* New York: Bantam Dell.

Isenhart, M., & Spangle, M. (2000). *Collaborative approaches to resolving conflict.* Thousand Oaks, CA: Sage.

Johnson, D., & Johnson, F. (1995). *Joining together: Group theory and group skills* (5th ed.). Boston: Allyn & Bacon.

Kegan, R., & Lahey, L. (2001). *How the way we talk can change the way we work.* San Francisco: Jossey-Bass.

McDonald, J., Mohr, N., Dichter, A., & McDonald, E. (2003). *The power of protocols: An educator's guide to better practice.* New York: Teachers College Press.

National School Reform Faculty. (2005). Protocols. Bloomington, IN: Harmony Education Center. www.nsrfharmony.org/resources.html

Patterson, K., Grenny, J., McMillan, R., Switzler, A., & Covey, S. (2007). *Crucial conversations: Tools for talking when stakes are high.* New York: McGraw-Hill.

Rees, F. (1991). *How to lead work teams: Facilitation skills.* San Francisco: Jossey-Bass/Pfeifer.

Schwarz, R. M. (1994). *The skilled facilitator: Practical wisdom for developing effective groups.* San Francisco: Jossey-Bass.

Tannen, D. (1995). *Talking from 9 to 5: Women and men in the workplace: Language, sex, and power.* New York: Avon.

Wheatley, M. (2002). *Turning to one another: Simple conversations to return hope to the future.* San Francisco: Berrett-Koehler.

THE INTRAPERSONAL DOMAIN

We look for works written by teacher leaders, principals, superintendents, and other educational leaders that capture the "inner dimensions" of leadership work. In addition to articles in professional journals, we draw upon the following:

Ackerman, R., & Mackenzie, S. (2007). *Uncovering teacher leadership: Essays and voices from the field.* Thousand Oaks, CA: Corwin.

Barth, R. (2000). *Learning by heart.* San Francisco: Jossey-Bass.

Donaldson, G. (Ed.). (1997). *On being a principal: The rewards and challenges of school leadership.* San Francisco: Jossey-Bass.

Donaldson, G., & Marnik, G. (Eds.). (1995). *As leaders learn: Personal stories of growth in school leadership.* Thousand Oaks, CA: Corwin.

Goleman, D. (1995). *Emotional intelligence.* New York: Bantam Books.

Holly, M. (1989). *Writing to grow: Keeping a personal and professional journal.* Portsmouth, NH: Heinemann.

Katzenmayer, M., & Moller, G. (2001). *Awakening the sleeping giant* (2nd ed.). Thousand Oaks, CA: Corwin.

Kidder, R. (2004). *Moral courage.* New York: HarperCollins.

Osterman, K., & Kottkamp, R. (1993). *Reflective practice for educators.* Thousand Oaks, CA: Corwin.

Palmer, P. (1997). *The courage to teach.* San Francisco: Jossey-Bass.

Shapiro, J., & Stefkovich, J. (Eds.). (2005). *Ethical leadership and decision-making in education.* Mahwah, NJ: Lawrence Erlbaum Associates.

Starratt, R. (2004). *Ethical leadership.* San Francisco: Jossey-Bass.

Van der Bogert, R. (Ed.). (1998). *Making learning communities work:* The critical role of leader as learner. San Francisco: Jossey-Bass.

ADULT AND PROFESSIONAL LEARNING

Most of our participants have had little exposure to adult learning theory and practice. They often find works dealing with professional learning and the development of competency and expertise very rewarding and affirming. Particularly for educational leaders, these resources can be tremendously valuable as leaders assist others at work with their own personal and professional learning. We recommend the following:

Argyris, C. (1991, April). Teaching smart people to learn. *Harvard Business Review, 69*(3), 99–109.

Argyris, C. (1993). *Knowledge for action.* San Francisco: Jossey-Bass.

Bloom, G., Castagna, C., Moir, E., & Warren, B. (2005). *Blended coaching: Skills and strategies to support principal development.* Thousand Oaks, CA: Corwin.

Boyatzis, R., Cowen, R., & Kolb, D. (1995). *Innovations in professional education: Steps on a journey from teaching to learning.* San Francisco: Jossey-Bass.

Brookfield, S. (1995). *Becoming a critically reflective teacher.* San Francisco: Jossey-Bass.

Donaldson, G., & Marnik, G. (1995). *Becoming better leaders.* Thousand Oaks, CA: Corwin.

Drago-Severson, E. (2004). *Helping teachers learn: Principal leadership for adult growth and development.* Thousand Oaks, CA: Corwin.

Goleman, D., Boyatzis, R., & McKee, A. (2002). *Primal leadership: Realizing the power of emotional intelligence.* Cambridge, MA: Harvard Business School Press.

Kegan, R., & Lahey, L. (2001). *How the way we talk can change the way we work.* San Francisco: Jossey-Bass.

Mezirow, J., and Associates (Eds.). (2000). *Learning as transformation: Critical perspectives on a theory in progress.* San Francisco: Jossey-Bass.

Senge, P., Cambron-McCabe, N., Lucas, T., Smith, B., Dutton, J., & Kleiner, A. (2000). *Schools that learn: A fifth discipline fieldbook.* New York: Doubleday.

Wenger, E. (1999). *Communities of practice: Learning, meaning, and identity.* Cambridge: Cambridge University Press.

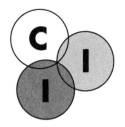

Index

About
the Author

GORDON A. DONALDSON, JR., has been learning about schools and how they can be led since he joined a teaching team at the Pennsylvania Advancement School in Philadelphia in 1967. His learning journey has taken him to other urban schools, in Philadelphia and in Boston; to a small island school on North Haven, Maine; to a small city district in Ellsworth, Maine; and finally, starting in 1979, to a variety of roles in leadership development programs in Maine and nationally. As readers of this book will know, his learning has been richly informed by his experience as a leader, by that of his colleagues, and by the growing literature that seeks to understand not simply how leadership *should* be performed, but also how it is learned and actually performed. Now a professor of education at the University of Maine, he lives with his wife, Cynthia, in Lamoine, Maine, a small community that helped them raise four children, who, not by chance, find themselves now working in the public interest—several in the vineyards of public education. He holds undergraduate and graduate degrees from Harvard University.